Calm Is Power

How to Stop Overthinking, Reduce Stress and Respond Better to Life

Nicole Hope Sylvester

Copyright © 2026 by Nicole Hope Sylvester

All rights reserved.

No part of this book may be reproduced, stored in a retrieval system, or transmitted in any form or by any means — electronic, mechanical, photocopying, recording, or otherwise — without prior written permission of the author, except in the case of brief quotations used in reviews or articles.

Published by Aligned Evolution Press.

First edition.

ISBN 979-8-9955418-0-6

Table of Contents

An Invitation

There was a time when I believed that if I just tried hard enough, I could keep up with everything life was asking of me.

But my body eventually told a different story.

This understanding didn't come to me in a peaceful moment of reflection. It arrived in the middle of a street, with my kids in the car, on a day that looked like every other day.

I was exhausted, running on responsibility and habit, ignoring every signal my body had been sending for months. Tension. Fatigue. Racing thoughts. The sense that I was always behind, no matter how fast I moved. I convinced myself this was normal. That this was what being a parent and an adult required.

One cold morning, just after picking my daughter up from preschool, I pulled up to a red light. For a moment, I closed my eyes. Just a breath. A brief pause, the sun warming my hands. When I opened them again, it was to the blaring sound of honking.

The light had already turned green. I had fallen asleep at the stoplight with my children in the back seat.

My body could no longer sustain the pace I was demanding from it. That moment wasn't me failing as a parent or a person. It was the signal — a clear message from my biology that I'd drifted far from my natural rhythm, and that the only option my body had left was to shut me down so I'd finally listen.

This book is the guide I wish I had in the years before that day.

A guide to understanding the real science and lived experience behind why we think the way we think, why we behave the way we behave, and why we keep repeating patterns that don't match the life we want.

This work brings together biology, beliefs, emotions, mindset and behavior so you can finally see the full picture of your internal world.

Not in a clinical way.

And not in a way that tries to perfect you.

But instead, in a human way — one that helps you understand yourself at the level where real change is possible.

Before you begin, there's something important to know.

This isn't a book you need to read in order — it's an intuitive book. Let your curiosity and your gut guide you.

You may find yourself drawn to a later chapter first. You may even discover that the final chapter is the best place to begin, because once you understand the power available when your body and mind work together, everything else lands more deeply.

You might choose a chapter based on your mood, a question you're carrying, or the part of your life you most want to understand right now.

There's no wrong place to enter this book. Every chapter reveals something essential about who you are and how your internal world actually works.

Along the way, you'll occasionally see short sections set apart from the main text. These asides are visually distinct, presented in italics and accompanied by the triangle symbol you see below. They offer additional perspective, context, or examples to deepen what you're learning.

An Attitude of Curiosity

The easiest way to move through these pages and really open to their concepts is through curiosity and wonder.

Curiosity about why certain reactions happen before you think. About whether the version of you that's been running your life is the one you intentionally chose. About the beliefs, sensations, emotional patterns, and inner logic that shape every decision, every relationship, every habit and every moment of your day.

When you become curious about yourself, you reclaim power you never realized you had.

My hope is that this book becomes something you return to again and again — one that sparks conversations with friends, invites you to journal alongside it and becomes a place for notes and reflection.

I hope it opens new, honest conversations with yourself. My goal is for it to feel like a companion that grows with you over time, one you can come back to as you change.

Your internal world is powerful, creative and magnetic when you understand how to work with it. This book is here to walk with you as that understanding deepens.

Start wherever you feel called. Follow your curiosity. Let this book meet you exactly where you are.

This is the beginning of your transformation, and wherever you enter is the perfect place to begin.

*A brief note before we move forward: The ideas and practices shared in this book are intended to support personal understanding and growth. They are not meant to replace professional medical or mental health care. If you are experiencing significant distress or need additional support, please reach out to a qualified healthcare professional

Chapter 1
The Power to Change Lies Within

The power to change your life doesn't begin in your environment or your thoughts. It begins in your body.

Your body isn't background noise in the change process.

It's your primary source of information, regulation and guidance.

When effort, discipline, and mindset alone fail to create lasting change, it's often because the body is overwhelmed rather than supported.

Calm isn't a mindset; it's a biological state.

And when the body is calm, its signals become clear rather than overwhelming.

From this foundation, clarity, choice and real agency become possible.

Everything else in this book builds from here.

Learning to Manage Life from the Inside Out

We all know, on some level, that life is made of change. Change happens around us every day. The seasons turn. Relationships evolve. Our bodies shift. Our priority lists rearrange themselves, sometimes without asking for permission. It often feels like the only thing we can count on is the sun rising in the morning and setting at night.

And yet, when the change we want is personal — our health, our relationships, our confidence, our work or the way we experience our own life — it often feels strangely out of reach.

For a long time, I believed that if I could just think better, try harder, and stay positive enough, something would finally click. I tried to think my way into joy. I tried to push myself out of overwhelm. I tried to build a better life with a determined mind while my body was holding a very different story. I kept returning to the same reactions, the same emotional loops and the same patterns I couldn't seem to outgrow. I truly believed mindset alone should be enough.

As it turns out, it wasn't.

What I eventually learned, after years of trial and error, is that the way I feel in my body isn't noise. It's information. My body was always telling me what was working, what was costing me, what felt aligned, and what was slowly wearing me down. I just didn't yet know how to listen to it in a useful way... or trust it.

I began to understand something many of us are never taught growing up. Calm and joy are not luxuries you earn through struggle or discipline. Joy is the feeling you get when you are being yourself and your life feels lined up with who you really are. And calm is what allows you to hear your body clearly so you can stay in alignment.

Most of us grow up learning that when something feels uncomfortable, the solution lives outside of us. We learn to try to change our circumstances, fix other people, or make life behave differently. And when that doesn't work, we learn to change ourselves instead.

We attempt to adjust our thinking, our behavior and even our personality to fit what the world expects. We become very good at coping, performing, and keeping things moving, often at the quiet cost of our own needs, truth and identity. We learn to manage life from the outside in.

But the power to change your life doesn't start in your environment. And that power doesn't start in your thoughts.

It begins in your body.

Life is short, and time is precious. Time spent understanding your internal world gives you years back. Years you may have spent walking a path that felt heavy, confusing, or disconnected. Years where the body was whispering that something felt off, but you didn't yet have the language to understand the message.

The power to change
begins within.

Every moment of overwhelm, every cycle of life when you thought you were failing, was really a signal pointing you toward a different way of living. A way that feels like clarity. A way that feels like choice. A way that feels like coming home to your truth.

This is why this journey matters. When you understand the intelligence inside your biology and beliefs, you unlock a level of freedom that changes everything. You become capable of choosing your next step with intention. You access an ease in life you may have never experienced before. And you start feeling confident that things will work out for you more often than not.

You begin to direct your life, not just navigate it.

A Note on Writing and Engaging With This Book

You'll get more from this book when you treat it as something you can interact with. Writing in these pages isn't required, but it is valuable.

When you put your thoughts on paper, your mind slows down, your body settles and your beliefs become visible. You begin to see what's living inside you instead of trying to hold it all in your head.

I was reminded of the value of this level of engagement by my daughter and her friend. One afternoon, they sat on the floor with a book designed to be scribbled on, torn and played with. They were laughing, exploring, learning and connecting without even realizing it.

That simple act of writing, doodling, and interacting with a book turned self-discovery into something fun, expressive and alive. It reminded me that learning is more powerful when it's embodied rather than passive. Sometimes the quickest way to understand yourself is through your hands, your senses and your willingness to play.

This book isn't meant to be destroyed, but it is absolutely meant to be *lived* in.

Write in the margins. Circle the sentences that open something in you. Add notes in the borders. Let the pages reflect your process. Connection grows when you put yourself on the page.

Here's your first moment of practice.

Reflection

Can you write in this book?

If your answer is yes, why?

If your answer is no, why?

What belief is shaping that choice?

Will you make a commitment to yourself in the border right now, declaring that you're ready for a life filled with more ease, happiness and connection?

(Simply by answering these questions, you are learning more about yourself, and that is the first step in the journey of awareness and self-empowerment.)

____

____

____

____

____

____

Chapter 2

The Human Operating System: How Your Life Is Shaped

Your Human Operating System is the way your body and mind work together to guide your life.

In this chapter, you'll learn how the Human Operating System (HOS) shapes your experience of life. You'll see how four core components — biology, beliefs, mindset, and behavior — work together to influence your thoughts, emotions and actions, and why understanding this system is the first step toward meaningful change.

I refer to your internal world as your **Human Operating System (HOS)**. Your Human Operating System is the way your body, subconscious patterns, emotions, thoughts and actions work together to shape how you experience your life.

To make this easier to understand, I describe your Human Operating System through four core components: **biology, beliefs, mindset and behavior.**

Biology is your body and nervous system. Beliefs reflect the subconscious and emotional meaning you carry about yourself and the world. Mindset is your conscious thinking and interpretation. Behavior is how all of this shows up in what you do.

I sometimes call these systems because each one follows its own patterns and rules. But they aren't separate parts. They're all part of one living system inside you, and they work together all the time. Each one affects the others as you move through your everyday life.

When one system is under strain, the others adapt around it. When the whole HOS is regulated (calm), all four work together with clarity, flexibility and ease. You know when this is happening because it feels really good.

What You Think Is "You" Is Actually Four Systems

Now that you've met the four core components of your HOS, there's something important to understand about them.

Most people walk through life believing they're steering the ship through conscious choice. You wake up and decide what to do. You choose how to respond, how to think, how to plan, and how to move through the day. It feels natural to assume that "you" are the one making every call.

But the truth is more layered — and once you understand it, far more liberating.

Much of what shapes your daily experience happens before conscious choice enters the picture. Your perceptions, reactions, decisions, and even the qualities you think of as personality are influenced by internal systems that work quietly in the background, guiding your thoughts and behavior before you ever notice yourself choosing anything.

Those systems — biology, beliefs, mindset and behavior — are constantly interacting beneath your awareness.

- Your biology sets your internal state before your mind forms a thought.
- Your beliefs filter your experiences and shape the meaning and emotions you attach to your circumstances.
- Your mind constantly creates stories based on your biology and beliefs, and those stories determine your next actions.
- Your behavior expresses whichever system is leading in that moment.

Most of us focus only on the last one. We notice what we did or didn't do, and we immediately evaluate ourselves through it. We worry about how others will interpret it and assume our behavior tells the whole story about us.

Behavior is simply the most visible system, so it becomes the one we try to control. We try to fix habits, strengthen discipline, or force motivation without realizing that behavior is only the final expression of everything happening underneath.

When you understand how these systems work together, you gain a clarity that feels like switching on the lights in a space you've lived in for years. You begin to see the patterns beneath your reactions and the origins of your thoughts. Things that once felt confusing or frustrating start to make sense in a new way.

We grow up being told to think differently, act differently, or try harder, yet no one gives us the internal blueprint that explains why we struggle. So we chase change at the surface while the deeper systems continue running the same patterns.

Understanding your Human Operating System doesn't make life effortless, but it gives you something even more valuable: awareness. Awareness opens the doorway to choice. Once you see the nature of these systems, you stop fighting yourself and begin working with the design of your own body and mind.

This is where transformation begins. Huzzah!

Reflection

Where in my life do I feel like I'm fighting myself?

Which system feels most familiar to me right now: biology, beliefs/emotions, mindset or behavior?

What do I hope becomes possible for me if I understand the forces shaping my reactions?

____

____

____

____

____

____

Another Way to See Your Internal World

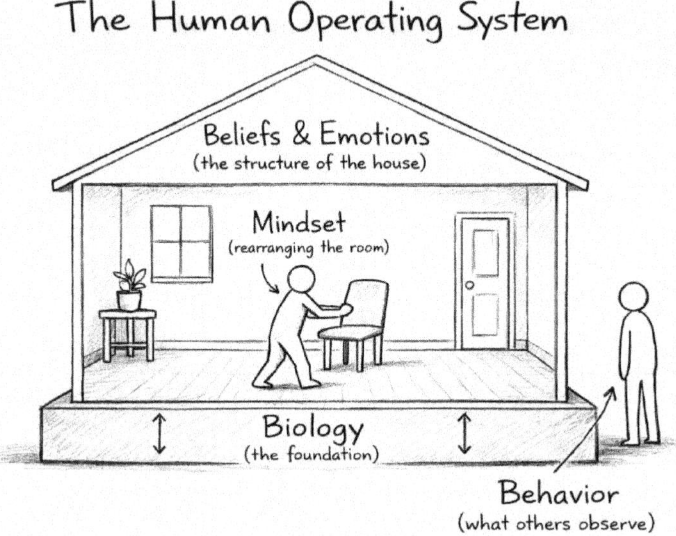

*Your **Human Operating System**, or HOS (hos, hows, hous... house), works a lot like a house you live inside every day.*

Biology is the foundation.

Biology, especially your nervous system, determines whether everything above it feels stable or strained. When the foundation is settled, the house can support movement, change and growth. When it's unsettled, nothing above it fully holds. You can paint the walls, open the windows, and rearrange every piece of furniture, yet the house still shakes.

A shaky foundation doesn't mean something's wrong with the house. It means the ground beneath it has been under pressure.

When your biology has been living in survival, the entire structure adapts around tension and unease. Floors creak. Doors stick. Rooms feel tight. Life feels harder than it needs to be because the base of the HOS is unstable.

This is why calm must begin in the body.

Stability starts at the foundation, and when the foundation steadies, everything above it finally has the chance to settle and expand.

Beliefs are the walls, the windows and the doors.

Beliefs shape the structure built on top of your foundation. They determine where the walls are placed and, in doing so, define how much internal space you experience yourself as having. They form the windows that decide what you are able to see, notice, and validate about the world beyond your house. And they become the doors that quietly decide where you feel safe enough to go, what you believe is possible and which parts of life feel accessible or subtly off-limits.

Aligned beliefs create rooms with air and light. They support movement, flexibility and growth. Fear-based beliefs narrow the structure. They reduce usable space, block natural sightlines (opportunities), and close access points (options), holding you inside patterns that feel normal simply because they have been reinforced for a long time.

Most beliefs are not consciously chosen. They're constructed gradually, often early in life, in direct response to what your nervous system needed in order to survive. Because of this, they tend to operate in the background, shaping perception and choice without ever being noticed.

Beliefs can expand the architecture of your life or gently limit it. And until you learn to recognize the structure they create, you may never realize how much space you were always capable of living inside.

Emotions are the building materials of beliefs.

Most core beliefs you carry began paired with a felt experience in your body. We usually call these felt experiences emotions — a real moment in the body that felt like fear, shame, relief, safety, confusion, pride, grief, or joy. Your nervous system uses those emotional, felt moments to build meaning about the world and about you.

That meaning becomes a belief. Those emotional states are what the nervous system uses to pour the concrete, raise the walls and reinforce the frame. The belief is the blueprint. The emotion is what makes it solid.

This is why beliefs rarely change just because you think differently. You can replace the words in your mind, but if the emotional memory in the body has not shifted, the structure underneath stays the same. The body is still holding the same frame.

When you begin to regulate your nervous system and allow emotions to move instead of being stored, you're not only creating calm, you're quietly loosening the very material that old beliefs were built from. And that's when the structure finally becomes flexible enough to change.

Mindset is how you try to create comfort and direction inside the house.

Your mind moves thoughts the way someone might move furniture, hoping the room will finally feel right. It reframes situations, reorganizes ideas and searches for better arrangements. This is the part of you that learns, plans, reflects and tries to improve your experience.

When the house feels stable, this works beautifully. The rooms have space. The foundation is steady. Rearranging actually changes how it feels to live there. From this place, the mind can also do something more powerful: it can open the door and explore life beyond the house.

This is the Wiser mind.

It's curious, creative, responsive, and able to choose rather than react.

When the foundation feels unsettled or the rooms feel tight from stress and emotional strain, the mind loses that freedom. Instead of exploring, it paces. Instead of imagining, it monitors. Instead of leaving the house, it keeps rearranging the same furniture again and again, hoping relief will come.

This is a survival response. The house doesn't feel safe enough to leave, so the mind stays inside trying to manage discomfort.

Which mind you're living from isn't decided by effort or discipline. It's decided by how safe your biology feels. A steady foundation gives the mind permission to rearrange with ease and, over time, to step outside the house and engage with life.

When the foundation is unsettled, the mind stays inside, working harder within the same walls, trying to make life feel manageable. Mindset alone doesn't create safety. Biological safety creates access to a growth-oriented mind, and from that place, life begins to expand.

Behavior is the part of the house that others can see.

It's how you move through the rooms, how quickly you pace (stress), where you linger (the habits you repeat) and what you avoid (denial). If your internal world were an ant farm, behavior would be the only thing visible from the outside.

People study your actions, your moods, your tone, and your habits, assuming that what they see is who you are. And very often, you use this same narrow view when judging yourself, like your intelligence, your capability and even your worth.

But behavior is never the whole story. It's simply the outward expression of the structure underneath. The foundation determines stability. The walls determine your capacity and your emotions. Behavior reflects how safe or strained it feels to live inside. When the house is steady, behavior looks calm, intentional and aligned. When the house is under pressure, behavior looks reactive, guarded or exhausted.

Behavior isn't the problem to fix. It's the signal pointing you back to the systems (biology, beliefs/emotions, mindset) beneath it.

A strong foundation creates a calm, spacious life. A spacious life allows the Wiser mind to lead. And the Wiser mind guides behavior that reflects your true self rather than your survival patterns.

This is the promise of this work. Calm strengthens the foundation so the whole house can expand, grow, and fully reflect who you are.

System 1 — Biology: The System That Decides First

Your biology begins shaping your experience before your conscious mind has a chance to respond. Your nervous system is always scanning for signals of safety or danger. It reacts with remarkable speed because its first priority is to keep you alive. Your body makes the first move, and your mind follows.

Many people assume their emotions begin with their thoughts. They believe clearer thinking will eventually lead to calmer feelings. But the body has its own intelligence. When your biology is tense, overwhelmed, exhausted, or over-emotional, your thoughts tend to match that state.

Calm biology supports clear thinking. Activated biology creates scattered, reactive thinking.

For many years, I wondered what was wrong with me because my anxiety never let up. I was eating well, teaching fitness classes and yoga, yet my body never felt healthy or relaxed. I was exhausted but could not fall asleep. I read books, followed mindfulness practices, and tried every mindset skill I could find. I showed up with real commitment. I worked hard to feel better. I worked hard to heal. Yet nothing created the lasting ease I was searching for.

My body kept determining my ability to enjoy life.

My breath stayed shallow, and my chest felt tight.

My throat closed without warning, which made eating difficult and somewhat scary.

My vision blurred under pressure, and my teeth ached from constant clenching.

My skin buzzed as if it wanted to leap off my bones, very uncomfortable.

I cried easily. I reacted quickly. I never felt truly rested, safe or happy.

My whole HOS lived on alert.

Anytime I felt relief, it didn't last long because the issue lived in my biology. My nervous system had adapted to a survival state years earlier, and I didn't recognize the pattern. The symptoms arrived slowly, disguised as separate problems. I treated them one by one and wondered why nothing created lasting relief.

It took me years to understand that the problem wasn't my mind or my discipline. The problem was the survival state my body had learned to normalize. Once I began listening to my biology and understanding the signals it had been sending all along, everything made sense.

Calm begins in the body, which means clarity begins there, too.

When the body settles, the mind opens.

When the body feels safe, new choices appear.

We probably should have expected this system to be sensitive. It's literally called the nervous system. Now we know just how accurate that name is.

Reflection

What's one body signal I often feel but rarely acknowledge?

What story do I tell myself about it?

What might change if I take action to calm my body sooner?

____

____

____

____

____

____

System 2 — Beliefs: The Invisible Rules That Shape Everything

If Biology decides first, then Beliefs are the behind-the-scenes system shaping how you interpret your life. They influence what you notice, what you expect and what you assume is possible. Many of these beliefs formed early through emotional experiences, quietly organizing your perceptions before you understood what you were learning. They become the lens through which you see yourself and the world around you.

A belief is a rule your body lives by. It's a repeated meaning that becomes integrated into how you respond and relate to life. Some beliefs support growth. Others limit what you allow yourself to experience.

Beliefs are closely tied to emotion. They aren't just thoughts, they're predictions your nervous system learned through experience. When a moment resembles something familiar, the body produces an emotional reaction first. The mind then interprets that reaction and assigns meaning. Over time, that meaning becomes a rule about how life works.

Because of this, people usually notice emotions before they recognize beliefs. The feeling appears immediately, while the belief shaping it remains invisible.

I worked with a client who had spent almost a decade doing everything they were told would lead to a better, happier life. Therapy, personal growth books, journaling, routines, workshops. They approached the work with sincerity and dedication, believing that effort and commitment would eventually bring relief.

Yet every new beginning fell apart the moment life challenged them.

As we explored together, one belief finally surfaced. They never would have identified it if I hadn't asked directly. It lived deep in their Belief system and shaped everything.

"Life is supposed to be hard, and I don't deserve to be happy."

One sentence.

A decade of outcomes.

That belief shaped how they approached change. It filtered every success. It erased evidence of progress. It tethered them to struggle even when life improved.

Beliefs aren't intellectual statements. They're survival rules written into the body. Until you see them, you live through them as if they are absolute truth.

When calm and curiosity become your baseline, these outdated beliefs rise with clarity. You begin seeing the stories you've carried and the rules you've lived under. You see where they came from and how they shaped you. And you gain the power to change them.

Understanding your beliefs helps you understand your patterns.

Understanding your patterns helps you understand your choices.

And understanding your choices helps you know your power.

Reflection

What's one belief that might be shaping my reactions to my life without my awareness?

___

___

___

___

___

___

System 3 — Mindset: The Part of You That Becomes Clear When the Body Is Ready

Mindset is the part of your HOS that allows you to direct your thoughts, choose a perspective, and interpret your experience with intention. It's powerful and transformative, but only when the rest of your internal world supports it.

The body sends far more information to the mind than the mind sends downward. This means most thoughts are responses to your internal state. When biology is activated and beliefs are protective, your thinking narrows. When your biology settles and your beliefs soften, your thinking opens. This is the beginning of clarity, and clarity means power.

This is also where the distinction between survival mind and Wiser mind becomes essential.

Survival mind reacts quickly, interprets life through pressure (fear) and focuses on getting through the moment. It's efficient, but it cannot reflect or consider new possibilities; it's tied to past experiences.

Wiser mind emerges when the body feels safe. It's spacious, creative, curious and capable of seeing beyond the immediate moment. This is the part of you that can think clearly and choose wisely. It allows you to consider other perspectives and see situations from a bird's-eye view.

Your mind is always creating stories and trying to determine your next step. The real question is whether those stories come from survival or from your Wiser mind.

Mindset practices work only when your internal world is steady enough to support clear, aligned, wiser thinking.

Reflection

What happens to my thinking when my body feels pressured?

Can I think of a time when my mind was stuck on a worry or fear, and I couldn't think about something else?

(This was a moment when your body was speaking louder than your Wiser mind. You will find tools for addressing this in the coming chapters.)

____

____

____

____

____

____

System 4 — Behavior: The Autopilot Behind Everything You Do

Behavior is the most visible part of the HOS, yet it's often the part we understand the least. We tend to treat behavior as a conscious choice. We assume discipline or motivation is what drives us. We blame ourselves when our actions don't match our intentions.

Behavior is also the part of us that we believe reveals who we truly are. This can make us overly critical of our actions and our presence, especially because behavior is the only part of our internal world that other people can actually see.

But most behavior is automatic.

Most behavior is patterned.

Most behavior runs on autopilot.

For years, I tried to discipline myself into being different. More productive. More calm. More confident. I created strict schedules. I organized every hour. I tried to control my way into a better life.

But my old patterns always returned because the systems underneath my behavior (especially my biology and my beliefs) had not changed.

Behavior reflects the internal system that is leading in that moment.

If your biology is overwhelmed, behavior follows.

If your beliefs are protective, behavior follows.

If your mindset is scattered, behavior follows.

Behavior doesn't tell you who you are. It tells you which system is driving the moment. The beginning of real change starts with self-awareness.

Reflection

What behavior patterns have I tried to change over the years but frustratingly return to?

____

____

____

____

____

____

The Interplay: Why Calm Changes Everything

These four systems work together constantly. They respond to each other, influence each other and shape your experience every moment of your life.

Calm is what helps your whole Human Operating System work together.

When your nervous system settles, your body uses less stress energy, your mind becomes clearer, and it becomes easier to make good choices. Instead of reacting automatically, you can pause and respond in a way that actually matches who you want to be.

This doesn't mean shutting down your feelings or trying to stay quiet and positive. It means your body feels safe enough to stay present, pay attention and connect with what is really happening.

From this steady state, you can notice what you feel, understand what you need and choose how you want to act.

As you start to understand these systems and learn how to work with them, you step into a level of clarity and personal power that feels like standing in the eye of a storm. Life can move in chaos, and you remain steady and sure-footed.

This is where your power lives.

Reflection

What does calm feel like in my body when I am truly focused on my body?

How does my thinking shift when calm is present?

____

____

____

____

____

____

Personal Power Practice

For the next day, notice your first reactions in stressful or uncertain moments or simply throughout your day.

Label each reaction with one word:

Biology

Beliefs

Mindset

Autopilot Behavior

Don't analyze. Don't judge. Just get curious and *simply notice*.

Awareness is the first step in learning to work with your HOS instead of against it.

To understand calm at its deepest level, we have to begin where calm actually begins: in the body itself.

Chapter 3

The Biology of Calm and the Nervous System

Your nervous system is the foundation of how you experience every moment of your life.

In this chapter, you'll learn how your nervous system shapes your reactions, emotions, and energy throughout the day — often before you're even aware of it.

You may start to recognize familiar patterns: overwhelm, a racing mind, low energy, or sudden waves of irritation or sadness. These aren't random experiences. They're signals from your body, and understanding them gives you a new way to work with what shows up each day.

Your nervous system decides safety, stress, and calm before your conscious mind has a chance to respond. Your body constantly scans your environment, your relationships, and your inner sensations to determine whether you can rest, connect and think clearly — or whether you need to protect and prepare.

Different nervous system states shape your emotions, thoughts, energy, health and behavior throughout the day. When stress becomes chronic, it changes both the body and the mind.

Understanding how your nervous system works gives you a practical way to recognize what state you're in — and what your body actually needs to return to calm.

Calm isn't something you think yourself into. Calm is something your body either allows or withholds based on what it perceives.

To access that calm, you first need to understand the system that creates it: your nervous system.

Your **nervous system** is your body's communication network. It gathers information, makes sense of what's happening around you and decides whether you're safe enough to relax or need to prepare for survival. It influences your heart rate, breathing, digestion, emotional tone and even the kinds of thoughts your brain is capable of producing.

One of the most important players in this system is the **vagus nerve**, a long and complex nerve that connects the brain to the heart, lungs, gut and immune system. It functions as a central messenger, constantly updating the body on whether it's safe to settle or needs to stay on guard.

Through this pathway, the nervous system helps regulate digestion, breathing patterns, muscle tone, inflammation and immune activity. When vagal signaling supports safety, the body shifts toward healing, balance and restoration. When those signals are disrupted by chronic stress or unresolved threat, the body organizes itself around protection instead.

This is why the effects of stress often appear in the body before they make sense in the mind. The same system shaping your emotional state is also shaping your physical health.

All of this is happening through a process called **neuroception**, your body's ability to detect safety or uncertainty before your conscious mind is aware. Neuroception operates faster than thought and faster than emotion. It evaluates subtle signals from your environment, your relationships, your memories, and your internal sensations, even the tone of someone's voice, before you form a single conscious interpretation.

When neuroception data reads as safe enough, your body naturally shifts toward regulation. The heart rate slows. Breathing deepens. Muscles begin to soften. Blood flow returns to the areas of the brain responsible for clarity, creativity and emotional intelligence. Without effort, your internal world becomes more available. Thinking widens. Perspective returns. Choice becomes possible again.

When neuroception reads uncertain, even for a brief moment, the body reorganizes in the opposite direction. Breathing lifts higher into the chest. Muscles brace. Stress chemistry rises (e.g., cortisol). The senses sharpen, and attention narrows. Thoughts shift, not because you decided to think differently, but because your biology has changed the range of thoughts your mind can access. The nervous system moves into protection mode.

For many years, I believed I could think my way into ease. I practiced meditation, repeated positive affirmations, explored mindfulness and applied every mindset tool I could find. None of it held. It wasn't because the tools were flawed, but because I was trying to build a calm mind on top of a body that was still living in survival mode.

Remember:

Your biology sets the conditions.

Your mind interprets them.

Your behavior reflects them.

This is why calm isn't optional. Calm is the entry point for everything else.

Reflection

Can I think of a moment when my thoughts couldn't calm my body?

____

____

____

____

____

____

Your Body Was Made to Scan for Bears

Your nervous system hasn't evolved for modern life.

It's evolved for survival.

For most of human history, the body had one job: stay alive long enough to see the next sunrise. That meant listening for danger, watching for threat, noticing every shift in the environment and reacting before thought could slow you down.

This ancient wiring still lives inside you.

Your biology is always scanning, always listening, always evaluating whether each moment feels safe enough for rest or requires some form of protection. It does this constantly, even when life looks calm on the outside.

In the wild, this scanning system had a clear job. Danger showed up, the body reacted, and once it was over, the body settled again.

Modern stress rarely ends like that. Work pressure, memories, relationships, money, parenting and poor sleep keep piling up. The body keeps watching everything and eventually stays in guard mode. Different experiences blend together, and everyday life starts to feel like danger.

It keeps looking.

It keeps preparing.

It keeps scanning for the next moment that might hurt emotionally or physically.

This is why your body can feel alert while you're driving, why your stomach tightens before reading a message, or why your mind speeds up when everything finally gets quiet. Your nervous system isn't overreacting. It's overworking. Over time, it has adapted to constant pressure and learned to stay prepared rather than allowing stress to rise and fall naturally with life.

Biology doesn't operate with nuance or interpretation. It reads the world through a simple lens: safe enough to relax or uncertain enough to prepare. When life remains uncertain for too long, the nervous system chooses preparation by default. It stays vigilant, predictive, and alert, even when no immediate threat is present. Calm begins to feel unfamiliar because your biology has forgotten how to rest. It starts to believe that the stress state is the safe state.

To make sense of your reactions, your patterns, and your capacity for ease, you need to understand how your body moves through different nervous system states — how activation builds over time and how overwhelm begins.

Your Nervous System Landscape

Before you learn what activation or shutdown feels like, you need to understand the landscape your nervous system moves through each day. Most people think the nervous system is either calm or stressed, but it's far more dynamic than that. It shifts constantly based on the signals it receives from your body and environment.

Your Nervous System Landscape

The Riverbank (Regulation)

The Ridge (Activation)

The Cave (Shutdown)

I imagine the nervous system as a landscape with three main zones. These are not levels you "level up" or "level down" into. They're states your body moves among depending on what it needs in the moment.

1. Regulation: The Riverbank (The Grounded Zone)

This is your natural home base.

Your biology is designed to spend most of its time here.

At the riverbank, your body can rest, digest, connect and create. This is where you gather "internal nourishment," clarity, energy, presence and the ability to think and choose. This is also where your body functions best to take care of itself, including digestion and immunity.

Your breath is steady and relaxed.

Your mind is clear and focused.

Your relationships feel easier.

You feel energized and like yourself.

This is where your Wiser mind is available.

Your system is always trying to return to this state.

2. Activation: The Mountain Ridge (The Mobilized-Stress Zone)

This state prepares you to take action for your survival.

It feels like racing up to a mountain ridge to scan for safety, where your body is working hard and your senses sharpen.

Your heart rate rises.

Your attention moves outward.

Your mind speeds up to keep you safe.

Activation is healthy in short bursts. It helps you solve problems, respond to challenges (danger) and move toward goals.

But if you keep running up and down the ridge without rest, you burn through your energy quickly.

And if you stay on the ridge too long, the ridge becomes your new living zone or "new normal."

Your mind and body begin scanning for danger constantly, even when nothing is wrong.

3. Shutdown: The Cave (The Conservation Zone)

When your system can no longer survive the ridge because it has become overwhelmed, it pulls you into the cave.

This is a protective state meant to conserve what's left of your energy.

Your body becomes heavy and tired.

Your mind feels distant and foggy.

Motivation fades.

This isn't collapse in a personal sense. It's protection in a biological sense. It's your system saying, "You've done too much for too long. Rest now."

But the cave isn't meant to be home either.

How Your System Moves Among the Zones

Your nervous system moves among these zones all day long. You may cycle through all of them before noon.

The riverbank is your natural home base. This is the state your biology was designed to return to again and again. It's where your body rests, builds immunity, digests and gathers the energy you need to live your life.

The ridge is where you mobilize energy for action.

The cave is where you recover when the system becomes overwhelmed.

Understanding this landscape helps you make sense of your reactions. It helps you stop blaming yourself for what is a biological response to life.

And it gives you the foundation you need for the tools that can give you relief.

Now that you understand the landscape, let's look at what happens in the first major shift away from the riverbank of calm regulation and rest to **activation**, your earliest signal that the nervous system is working hard to protect you.

When Life Feels Like Too Much: The Biology of Activation

When your nervous system shifts into activation — stress mode — every sense raises its awareness. Hearing becomes more alert. Vision narrows or darts as your eyes scan for cues. Thoughts begin to move faster, trying to calculate possibilities, predict outcomes, and stay one step ahead. Internally, it can feel like pushing up to a mountain ridge, higher and higher, for a better view of what might be coming.

This isn't psychological. It is physiological. It's the function of the sympathetic branch of the nervous system, designed to mobilize energy when the body senses possible threat. From the perspective of your biology, something feels uncertain, and preparation becomes necessary. In very simple terms, your system is acting as if a bear might be nearby.

Activation can be triggered by many things that aren't physically dangerous: a tone of voice, an unexpected message, a sudden change in plans, a memory rising to the surface. In response, the body releases stress chemistry like cortisol and adrenaline to prepare you for action. Heart rate increases. Breathing becomes quicker. Muscles tighten, especially in the hips and shoulders. The senses kick up to go mode.

The world becomes louder (sounds, light, texture, smells). This heightened awareness is your biology trying to keep you alive. Again, your body was only meant to stay activated for a short period of time and then return to its calm and happy state.

The tricky piece is that modern life has become more and more complicated and chaotic, resulting in the body holding a state of activation (stress) longer and more frequently. This is chronic stress, which is rapidly becoming the norm rather than the exception.

This constant activation can feel like:

- Anxiety
- Urgency
- Irritation
- Restlessness
- Hyperplanning
- Confusion mixed with speed

The challenge is that activation is expensive. Living on the mountain ridge burns through energy quickly. It taxes focus, emotional capacity and physical reserves. The nervous system isn't designed to stay mobilized indefinitely. When activation continues without enough relief, the body begins searching for another strategy, one that conserves energy instead of spending it.

That doorway leads to overwhelm and shutdown. But prolonged activation always comes first.

Reflection

What does early activation feel like in my body? Irritability? Anxiety?

Do I feel "stressed" or "overly emotional"?

Am I constantly trying to predict multiple outcomes or hyper-prepare for what is coming in the future?

____

____

____

____

____

____

When Stress and Overwhelm Last Too Long, Your Nervous System Begins to Shut Down

After prolonged activation, the nervous system shifts from intensity into withdrawal. This is often experienced as shutdown, the move from the mountain ridge into the cave. It isn't a conscious choice. It's the body's attempt to preserve what energy remains.

This state is associated with the dorsal vagal branch of the vagus nerve, the most ancient protective response in the nervous system (think lizards). When the system determines that mobilization is no longer sustainable, it conserves resources by reducing engagement with the world.

The shift usually happens gradually. Energy starts to drop. Taste and appetite can diminish, the senses dampen and motivation fades. Mood changes from sharp and reactive to heavy or distant, and connection can feel harder to access, even when you want it.

This state can feel like living at a distance from your own life.

I lived here for a long time without recognizing it. I thought I was simply tired. I assumed I was low-energy or emotionally off. I wondered if something was wrong with me, physically or psychologically. But what was actually happening was simpler and more sobering: my system had been activated for so long that it no longer had the capacity to stay on the ridge.

The cave became the only option left. I found myself treating my bed like a shelter, returning to it whenever I could, drawn to the sense of enclosure and relief it offered.

Medical tests told me everything was fine. My body told a different story.

Acupuncture was the first moment I experienced a real shift. Not because it fixed everything, but because it gave my nervous system a brief window of safety and relief. That small window was enough for regulation to return. Colors appeared brighter. Sound felt clearer. I wanted connection again. Life felt reachable.

Shutdown isn't a failure of the system. It's protection. It's the nervous system's last resort when stress has gone on for too long.

And when relief arrives, even briefly, the world becomes livable again.

Reflection

Have I ever mistaken shutdown for lack of motivation or personality, when it was actually my system trying to protect me?

____

____

____

____

____

____

What Chronic Stress Looks Like in the Body

Stress isn't just a feeling. It's a biological state.

When the nervous system stays in protection mode for too long, the body begins to show clear, predictable signs. Not because something's broken, but because energy is being redirected toward survival instead of repair.

Chronic stress often shows up as:

- Digestive issues such as bloating, cramping, IBS or appetite changes
- Skin reactions like rashes, sensitivity or unexplained breakouts
- Ongoing inflammation, including joint pain, muscle tension or water retention
- Hormonal shifts that affect mood, energy or sleep
- A weakened or overactive immune system leading to frequent illness
- Shallow or disrupted sleep

- Reliance on caffeine or sugar just to get through the day

These symptoms may seem unrelated, but they share the same root cause: a nervous system that's been working too hard for too long.

This is what stress becomes when it isn't resolved. It may feel like drama, weakness, or failure. But it's actually **dis-ease**: the gradual loss of ease inside the body.

When the body lives in prolonged survival mode, balance becomes harder to maintain. Over time, chronic stress has been strongly associated with serious health conditions such as heart disease, diabetes, and some forms of cancer, not because stress is the sole cause, but because the body requires regulation and recovery to repair, restore and function well.

A system that's constantly defending has fewer resources available for healing — and fewer resources available for life. Patience shortens. Focus fragments. Emotional flexibility narrows. It becomes harder to show up as the parent, partner, or professional you want to be.

Health depends on balance, not only in the body, but in how we relate to the people and responsibilities that matter most. Chronic stress starts eroding that balance before symptoms are labeled or diagnosed.

Reflection

Which of these signals does my body use to tell me it's been in protection mode for too long?

____

____

____

____

____

____

What Chronic Stress Feels Like in the Mind and Emotions

While the body carries the physical load, the mind and emotions change too.

In the mind, chronic stress can look like:

- Thoughts that go in circles and are hard to shut off
- Trouble focusing or remembering things
- Decision-making feels harder than it should
- Constant planning, worrying, or replaying conversations
- Feeling busy in your head, but not actually getting much done
- Rest that doesn't feel restful, like you should be doing something else

Emotionally, chronic stress can feel like:

- Getting irritated or overwhelmed more easily
- Feeling impatient, snappy, or emotionally tired

- Small problems feeling bigger than they really are
- Joy or excitement fading quickly instead of lasting
- Feeling flat, numb, or emotionally muted at times
- Less access to curiosity, creativity, or playfulness

Over time, stress can even change how you relate to yourself:

- Not knowing what you want or how you feel
- Doubting your own instincts or decisions
- Feeling responsible for everything and everyone
- Calm feeling strange or uncomfortable
- Quiet moments bringing restlessness instead of relief

There can be other influences, but for many people, these patterns reflect a nervous system that hasn't had enough opportunity to fully rest and reset. When the nervous system stays in protection mode, it has less energy available for connection, patience and curiosity. The body shifts into autopilot, and reactions begin to replace thoughtful responses.

It becomes harder to show up fully as a parent, partner, or professional, not because you don't care, but because your system is worn down. You may want to respond differently, but the capacity simply isn't there in the moment.

Health and wellbeing depend on balance, not only in the body, but in how we think, feel, relate and respond to life. Over time, chronic stress pulls you out of balance long before anything is named, labeled, or diagnosed.

What Calm Restores

Calm isn't a reward for getting life right. It's the biological state that allows the body to function as intended.

When the nervous system receives enough signals of safety, the body shifts out of defense and back into regulation. Energy that was being spent on protection becomes available for repair, balance and clarity.

In a consistently regulated state, the benefits ripple outward:

- The brain regains access to learning, planning and decision-making
- Inflammation decreases, and the body recovers more efficiently
- Digestion, immune function and sleep stabilize
- Emotions become easier to manage, and feeling good becomes the norm rather than the exception
- New habits and patterns become possible

But the shift doesn't stop inside the body.

When your biology is calm, you show up differently in the world. You listen better. You react less. You make clearer decisions. You have more patience with your children, more presence with your partner, and more capacity at work. You are driven less by urgency and guided more by intention.

This is why calm changes everything. Life doesn't suddenly become perfect, but you regain access to the internal resources that allow you to meet life with resilience.

Calm restores the biological conditions that make health, connection, confidence and fulfillment possible.

Why We Start With the Body

Most approaches try to create change through thought alone: mindset, motivation, or self-talk. These tools are useful, but they work more effectively *after* the body feels safe enough to support them.

The nervous system sets the state first. The mind responds second. If the body is in protection mode, the brain is limited to survival priorities. No amount of positive thinking can override that biology. But physical signals can.

Simple, body-based cues communicate safety directly to the nervous system, allowing it to downshift out of defense. Once that happens, clarity returns and mental tools actually work.

This is why the work starts with the body. Not because thoughts don't matter, but because biology decides whether thoughts will really help.

In the next section, you'll learn a small set of physical tools designed to cue safety quickly and gently. These tools don't replace insight or mindset. They make them possible.

Calming Tools: How to Know a Tool Is Working

Before we get into specific tools, it helps to know what you're actually looking for. When a tool begins to calm your system, your body will give you small automatic signals — not dramatic ones, just quiet shifts that happen on their own.

You might notice:

- a deeper breath
- a natural sigh or yawn
- a swallow
- a tiny burp
- a softening somewhere in your body (shoulders, jaw, hips)

These are signs your vagus nerve is responding, and that it is moving out of protection and back toward regulation.

You don't need to force anything. Just use the tool until one of these cues shows up. That's your body saying, *"Okay, I'm settling."*

As for *when* to use these tools, the answer is simple and practical. Use them often. Not only when you're overwhelmed or already stressed, but at the *very first* hint that something feels off. That slight edge. That subtle tightness in your face or shoulders. That moment when you notice yourself bracing, rushing, or mentally scanning anything that feels defensive.

Think of calm like standing on the riverbank. When you stay there, you can see clearly, respond thoughtfully and feel in flow. These tools help you stay on the riverbank. If you wait until you've already run up the mountainside of stress, it takes more valuable energy to come back down.

These practices aren't just for recovery. They're for maintenance. They help your system learn that calm is something you return to again and again, not something you fall out of and scramble to regain.

Now let's begin with three simple tools that speak directly to the body and help create calm from the inside out.

Tool: Orienting with Your Eyes

A 10–20 second reset for an activated mind.

When animals return to safety, the first thing they do is look around.

This is a biological cue that says, "The danger passed."

Your nervous system responds the same way.

How to Do It:

1. SIt or stand comfortably.
2. Gently move your eyes to the far right and pause for 2–3 seconds.
3. Move your eyes to the far left and pause again.
4. Then let your eyes scan the room slowly, landing on a few objects. (You can even choose your favorite color to help narrow down your search.)
5. Let your breath follow naturally. Repeat until you feel calm kick in, even just a little.

Why It Works:

Side-to-side eye movement engages the vagus nerve and lowers sympathetic charge.

Scanning the room tells your system you are not in danger right now.

This is one of the fastest ways to interrupt activation.

(You can even practice this with your eyes closed, as you try to fall asleep. Of course, you can't "see" anything in the dark with your eyes closed, so just pretend to see the room.)

Tool: Hand-To-Heart + Slow Breaths

A direct signal of safety through the heart and diaphragm.

Your body responds to warmth, pressure and slow exhalation. These cues activate the part of the vagus nerve responsible for calming and reconnecting you to the present moment.

How to Do It:

1. Place and gently press one hand on your chest.
2. Place the other hand on your lower ribs or belly.
3. Inhale gently through your nose.
4. Exhale longer than your inhale, even by one second.
5. Let your hands remind your body that you are safe enough to calm a little. Repeat as long as necessary.

Why It Works:

Touch communicates safety faster than language. A longer exhale activates the calming branch of the vagus nerve. Together, they create a physiological shift toward regulation.

This is a powerful tool when negative emotions rise quickly.

Tool: Centering Through Your Feet

A grounding practice that brings your system back into the present moment.

Your feet have dense nerve endings that communicate directly with your balance and stability systems. Gentle movement here restores a sense of orientation, "I am here. I am supported."

How to Do It:

1. Stand and feel the weight of your feet on the ground.
2. Slowly roll from heel to toe.
3. Then roll side to side, noticing pressure change.

4. Let your breath settle as your body finds balance.

Why It Works:

Grounding through the feet interrupts spiraling thoughts, pulls attention out of the future and reorients your nervous system to the present moment.

It's subtle but deeply stabilizing — especially when thoughts are racing.

You'll find a full description of these tools again in the **Toolbox section at the back of the book.*

These three are your starting point; the first signals that teach your biology how to return to the riverbank.

Small moments of regulation repeated often are what create lasting calm.

What Becomes Visible When You Settle

As your body settles and your system shifts out of protection, something subtle and powerful begins to happen. You start to notice your thoughts again, not just the loud ones, but the quieter ones underneath. You may catch yourself reacting and suddenly wonder, *Why did I think that? Why did I assume that? Why does this feel true in my body?*

As your body settles, you begin to uncover the beliefs that have been steering your life without your permission.

This is where curiosity and growth can create real change. Not in forcing new thoughts, but in finally seeing the ones that have been running quietly in the background.

It's hard to shift a belief from a survival state. But from regulation, the mind becomes flexible again. Beliefs loosen their grip. What once felt like truth begins to feel like information.

This is the doorway into the next chapter.

We'll explore the beliefs that shaped you, the beliefs that guide you now, and how beliefs and emotions work together to direct your reactions and choices. With calm as your foundation, you'll finally have the agency to decide which beliefs you keep and which ones you're ready to outgrow.

Reflection

After practicing one (or more) of the above tools, ask yourself:

Did it help?

Which one worked best?

When can I start using these Calming Tools to push the calm button on my nervous system?

____

____

____

____

____

____

The Basic Healthy Choices That Support Your Nervous System

As you begin using the tools in this chapter, it helps to remember something very simple:

Your nervous system is supported by how you live and how you take care of your physical body.

Food matters.
Your brain and nervous system run on real fuel. Regular meals, steady blood sugar and enough nourishment signal stability to the body. When your body is underfed or constantly running on empty, your system reads uncertainty.

Water matters.
Even mild dehydration increases physical stress inside the body and makes regulation harder than it needs to be.

Sleep matters.
Rest isn't only recovery for your mind. It's the state in which your nervous system repairs, resets and restores balance. Consistent sleep is one of the strongest biological signals of safety.

Movement and elimination matter.
Gentle movement, stretching, and simply allowing your body to go to the bathroom when it needs to are part of how the nervous system releases load. Holding, rushing, and overriding body cues keep the system stressed and break down the relationship between mind and body.

Connection matters.

Your nervous system was built to regulate with other nervous systems. This is called co-regulation. A safe conversation, shared laughter, eye contact, touch, or simply being around someone who feels grounded can settle your system faster than any technique.

Environment matters.

Light, sound, temperature, and the pace of your surroundings shape how your body feels. Calm is easier when your environment supports your nervous system instead of constantly demanding from it.

These aren't "lifestyle extras." They're how you take care of your body so it can work the way it was made to. The tools in this book work best when your body is being cared for and getting what it needs. When your body knows its most basic needs will be met, it feels safer. And when the body feels safer, calm becomes easier to find again.

Chapter 4
The Architecture of Belief

Beliefs are the internal rules your body learned through emotional experience.

This chapter explains how beliefs form as internal rules — often early in life — through repeated emotional patterns in your environment. You'll learn the difference between **survival beliefs** (automatic, protective, familiar) and aligned beliefs (chosen with calm and clarity), and explore the three core survival belief categories: safety, worth and power.

You'll also see how emotions reveal which belief is running in the moment, and how calm helps you update old rules so they support who you're becoming.

Most people assume beliefs are thoughts they picked up along the way, ideas they agreed with, adopted, or decided were true. But beliefs run much deeper than that. A belief is the internal rule your HOS uses to understand the world. It organizes how you respond, what you protect, what you hope for, and how you make sense of yourself in any moment.

What's surprising to most people is that very few beliefs were consciously chosen. The majority were created as emotional survival rules, instinctive patterns your body formed to stay connected and remain "part of" the world you grew up in. These rules took shape before you had language to question them or logic to compare or choose differently.

Your body learned who to be and how to move through your environment by feeling its way through tone, tension, attention, distance, unpredictability and affection. It wasn't thinking; it was adapting.

These early rules are what I call survival beliefs. They weren't formed through reflection or deliberate choice. They took shape through the emotional patterns and behaviors around you, the subtle and not-so-subtle experiences that taught your body how to maintain closeness, avoid conflict and read the adults you depended on.

Because these beliefs were adopted and created so early and repeated so consistently, they don't feel optional. They feel like truth, even when they're simply old instructions your HOS has never had a reason to question.

Under stress, these survival beliefs take the lead. They activate quickly and quietly, shaping your reactions before you have time to register what's happening. They influence how you read someone's tone, how you anticipate rejection or approval, how you manage uncertainty, and what you assume about your own worth or capability.

There's another category of belief, though, one that becomes more easily available in adulthood. **Aligned beliefs**, which are the *beliefs you choose* with clarity and self-awareness rather than urgency. They come from a grounded sense of who you're becoming, not the child you once needed to be. These beliefs take shape when your HOS is calm enough to see the present moment without filtering it through the emotional rules of your past. They grow in the space where you feel safe enough to tell the truth about what you want and steady enough to act on it.

This chapter brings these pieces together so you can finally see why certain reactions feel automatic, why familiar patterns repeat themselves even when you know better, and why shifting beliefs often feels harder than it sounds. When you understand the origin of these rules, it becomes easier to work with your system instead of fighting it.

You're about to see the emotional, belief blueprint your body has been following, possibly for decades, and you'll learn how to update it so it supports the life you're building now. The first step is understanding the difference between the beliefs you're calmly and consciously choosing today and the survival beliefs your body created before choice was even possible.

To begin that shift, we start at the foundation: the early rules your belief system built before you had any idea what a belief was.

What Survival Beliefs Are (And Why You Have Them)

As mentioned, most survival beliefs are the emotional rules your belief system created when you were young. They sit beneath your thinking mind and shape the way you interpret the world, often without your awareness.

What makes these beliefs unique is that they were formed during a time when your body was your primary guide. Your nervous system was learning how to stay connected, how to read the environment, and how to predict the emotional shifts of the people you depended on.

A survival belief isn't formed through a single moment. It forms through repetition. Your system feels the same emotional pattern again and again, maybe tension, maybe inconsistency, maybe pressure to perform or stay small, and it begins to organize your behavior around what keeps you most regulated (feeling safe). These patterns become internal rules: *this is how I stay close, this is how I avoid conflict, this is how I stay safe enough to belong and feel loved.*

They live in the body as instinct, not as language.

Because these beliefs were created so early, they don't feel optional. They feel like the natural way things work. They feel like *you*. But they're simply the first set of instructions your nervous system wrote when it was trying to understand a world much bigger than you had the capacity to process.

An example of one of the earliest rules a child learns is deeply relational:

If the people around me are not okay (happy, pleased), then I am not okay.

This rule is rarely spoken. It's sensed. A child notices the shift in a parent's expression, the heaviness of the room, a quick change in tone — even words — and the body responds immediately. The nervous system begins to link its own safety to the emotional state of others. And once that link is formed, the body carries it into adulthood unless something interrupts the pattern.

I carried that belief for years. I could sense tension before anyone said a word. My HOS treated other people's emotions as my responsibility, as if my own ease depended on fixing whatever they were feeling. That rule shaped my personality more than any conscious choice ever did. It taught me to stay pleasant, to minimize my needs, to avoid confrontation and to adjust myself to whatever made the room feel lighter.

This is the nature of survival beliefs. They once protected you, and later they limit you. They guide your behavior without asking permission. They influence how you show up in relationships, how you handle stress, how you navigate work, and even how you hold your body during conflict. And because they're familiar, they're rarely questioned.

The most important thing to understand is this:

Beliefs are practiced decisions.

Survival beliefs are the ones you practiced before you had the ability to make the decision.

Your body created them based on what it felt, not what it understood. It learned safety by patterned experiences, not explanation. And those patterns can stay active for years after the original circumstances are gone.

The work you'll do in this chapter will help you recognize those old rules, meet them with calm, and begin choosing beliefs that match the life you're building now, not the life you had to navigate as a child.

Reflection

Can I think of moments in my life where I felt responsible for holding the peace? Is it possible that I've been "keeping the peace" since childhood?

Which of my adult patterns make more sense when I remember what my younger self needed to do to feel loved and connected?

____

____

____

____

____

____

The Neuroscience of Patterned (Survival) Beliefs

Neuroscience is the science of how your brain and nervous system work: how you think, feel, learn, remember, and react. It studies the "wiring" inside you: the brain, the spinal cord and the nerve cells that send signals throughout your entire body.

In simple terms, neuroscience helps explain why you feel what you feel, why some reactions happen before you think, and why certain patterns follow you even when you want them to change. It reveals the framework behind your emotions, your habits and your automatic behaviors.

Here's the part that matters most for this work: **your brain doesn't give your conscious mind the full story.**

Most of what you react to each day comes from your subconscious, the part of your brain that runs old patterns automatically. It reacts before you can reason, choose, or understand what's happening.

Your subconscious is fast. It scans your environment constantly and filters almost everything before it reaches your awareness. It decides what you notice and what you ignore. It decides what feels safe and what feels threatening. And it bases those decisions on the emotional rules your nervous system learned in childhood.

You aren't reacting to the moment itself. You're reacting to what your brain *predicts* the moment means — and your brain loves predicting because that means control and survival.

Your brain takes in around eleven million bits of information every second, but your conscious mind can only handle about forty. The rest gets filtered out. And the filter is shaped by the beliefs your body practiced first.

Your brain isn't trying to give you an accurate picture of reality. It's trying to give you a familiar one. This is how predictive coding works: the brain uses the past to interpret the present because prediction feels faster and safer than uncertainty.

This is why a belief can feel true even when your logic disagrees.

This is why mindset alone doesn't calm you down.

This is why old emotional rules override your best intentions.

But if your body holds a different belief, it will look for evidence to prove it. This is **confirmation bias.** It is happening inside your nervous system. Your body highlights what matches old beliefs and filters out what does not. For example, you could receive a dozen moments of positive validation... but if you believe you are not enough, your attention will hook onto the one negative comment.

It's like wearing sunglasses with tiny holes punched in the lenses. You only see the parts of life that match your old emotional rules. Everything else dims in the background.

My strongest patterned belief was abandonment. A delayed text or a distracted tone could tense my body instantly. My mind was capable of offering reasonable explanations, but my body reacted first, with unease and sometimes panic, before my thoughts caught up. My HOS wasn't responding to the present moment. It was responding to a prediction it had rehearsed for years: that connection would disappear and that I was somehow unworthy of being chosen or stayed with.

When you understand this internal dynamic, everything begins to make sense. The reactions you once judged or were confused by seem more understandable. The patterns you thought were personal flaws become easier to shift. They were survival strategies created when you had fewer tools and far less support. They simply outlasted the environment that required them.

Here's the best news, though: your nervous system isn't fixed.

What it learned in protection can be relearned in safety. When the body settles, old beliefs lose their urgency, and new expectations become available.

Reflection

Take this slowly. Looking at your beliefs isn't about judging yourself; it's about meeting your inner world with neutrality and curiosity. When you can spot an old belief that's still shaping your reactions or your choices, you gain something powerful: relief.

You begin to see that many of the limits you feel today were created in another time, for another version of you. And once you can see them, you're no longer held inside the old rules. You create space for more confidence, more clarity, and a life that feels more aligned with who you're becoming.

Ask yourself:

Where do I see my past shaping how I interpret what's happening right now?

What situations seem to bring up the same emotional pattern again and again?

What belief might my body be holding onto to protect me... even if it no longer fits the life I'm living now?

____

____

____

____

____

____

The Three Core Survival Beliefs

(The Zoo Model of Human Psychology)

To understand why your reactions feel so automatic today, imagine what it would be like to be born inside a zoo.

A baby animal born in a zoo doesn't know anything about the outside world. It only knows the environment it wakes up in: the enclosure, the keepers, the routines, the expectations, and the other animals it shares space with. Everything it learns about "how life works" comes from inside that small world.

You were no different.

Your childhood was your first enclosure — your zoo.

Not because anyone intended to confine you, but because it was the only world you had access to. You learned how to survive, how to behave, and how to get your needs met by watching the people around you and responding to the emotional atmosphere they created.

And just like a young animal, you learned the rules quickly:

- which behaviors kept things calm
- what created tension, disapproval or negative consequences
- how to approach the "keepers" (the adults that were taking care of you)
- how to interact with the other "animals" in your space
- what earned attention or comfort, and what quietly closed the door

None of this was conscious. Your nervous system was gathering information, moment by moment, building a sense of how life works.

A baby animal in the zoo learns how much noise is allowed, when to stay close, when to give space, and which behaviors lead to better care. It knows this zoo is its world, so it adapts to fit it.

You did the same.

Your zoo taught you:

- which emotions were safe to show
- which parts of yourself needed to stay quiet or hidden
- what brought connection
- what created conflict or punishment
- what earned approval or care
- what led to withdrawal or overwhelm

This enclosure became your micro-world, and your nervous system treated it as the *template for life*. The rules you learned there became the default map your brain uses to navigate relationships, conflict, opportunities, and emotional safety, even after you leave the zoo.

From this map, your system formed instinctive beliefs, survival strategies shaped through repetition, not thought. Underneath each one were three essential questions your body was constantly answering:

Am I safe here?

Am I valued here?

Do I have influence here?

These questions became the foundation for the three core survival beliefs:

Safety

Worth

Power

These beliefs shaped the architecture of your inner world. They told you what to expect, what to fear, what to pursue, and who you needed to be in order to belong inside the enclosure you started in.

Now, let's explore each one.

1. Safety Beliefs: "Am I safe in this environment?"

Safety beliefs are the earliest to form because, for a child, safety is survival. Before you had language, your nervous system was already asking one constant question: **"Am I safe in this moment?"**

A young child can't separate emotional instability from actual danger. The body treats them as the same thing. When a parent comes home overwhelmed or tense, a child's system doesn't think, "They had a long day." It feels a shift in the environment and responds as if something has become uncertain. When a caregiver withdraws or shuts down, it doesn't register as distance; it registers as a loss of safety.

In early life, safety isn't created by explanations; it's created by **coregulation**. A child's nervous system stabilizes through the nervous system of the adult caring for them. When the parent is calm, the child's body softens into regulation. When the parent is stressed, distracted, overloaded, or emotionally unavailable, the child's system stays on alert because there is no external anchor.

Your body learned safety through the bodies around you.

And when the adults in your "zoo" were inconsistent, overwhelmed, or unable to regulate themselves, your belief system adapted. It began creating rules to help you survive emotionally overwhelming moments.

You learned, without a single word being spoken:

- pay attention to the emotional atmosphere
- track tiny shifts in tone
- listen for changes in rhythm, volume, or silence
- read facial cues before behavior
- anticipate what might come next

This wasn't anxiety. It was **pattern recognition** in a nervous system that had not yet developed the power to protect itself.

Your nervous system and belief system became a prediction machine because prediction felt safer than surprise. Staying one step ahead reduced the risk of emotional shock or perceived threat. Anticipation became protection.

This is where fear of rejection begins. Not as a fear of "not being liked," but as a fear of losing safety and protection, what many people later come to call love. When someone pulls away, says no, or becomes unpredictable, your body doesn't experience it as a small social disruption. It registers it as a threat to belonging.

Rejection hits the nervous system hard because, biologically, exclusion once meant danger. Being pushed out of the group reduced access to food, protection and survival itself. The brain processes social rejection through the same pain pathways as physical injury, which is why rejection can feel sharp, immediate and overwhelming. Even our language reflects this. We say we were "burned" by someone because the body experiences it that way.

So the belief isn't, *"They don't care."*

The belief becomes, *"If I lose connection, I lose safety."*

Safety beliefs live deeper than thought.

They activate before logic.

And they quietly shape the background filter of your emotional life.

Reflection

Can I sense how my body learned to equate connection with safety?

When and where in my life did closeness feel essential to survival and distance feel threatening?

You don't need solutions yet. Awareness is enough.

____

____

____

____

____

____

2. Worth Beliefs: "Am I valuable enough to stay connected and alive?"

Worth beliefs form next. They shape how you understand your emotional place in the world.

These beliefs develop as your HOS learns to link your behavior to whether people move toward you or away from you. Without words, you were noticing:

- which feelings brought closeness

- which needs created discomfort
- which behaviors earned attention
- which brought distance
- which parts of you were welcomed
- which parts were labeled "too much" or "not enough"

None of this was taught directly. You learned it through sensation, timing and repetition. Through the way faces changed. Through tone shifts. Through who stayed and who pulled back. Your nervous system and belief system worked together to draw conclusions about what was safe to express and what needed to be managed, hidden, or reshaped.

These conclusions became worth beliefs, internal rules about how to remain connected in the world.

If abandonment beliefs answer the question, *"Will I be left?",* worth beliefs answer a different one: *"Who do I need to be to stay?"*

For some people, this becomes the birthplace of people-pleasing. The HOS concludes, *"If the people around me don't feel okay, I'm not okay either."*

So you adapt. You learn to read the emotional weather and adjust yourself accordingly. If someone is stressed, you lighten the room. If someone is sad, you move into comfort. If the atmosphere tightens, your body shifts into the version of you that makes things easier for everyone else, even if it means setting your own emotions aside.

Over time, these responses stop feeling like strategies.

They start to feel like identity.

For others, worth beliefs take a different shape. You learn to be impressive instead of expressive. Independent instead of connected. Useful instead of honest. Low maintenance instead of needing. High functioning instead of present.

The form varies, but the logic is the same.

For me, these beliefs became so familiar that they almost felt like old friends. I even bragged about my ability to "chameleon" into whoever people needed me to be. I wore it like a badge of emotional intelligence, believing it meant I was adaptable, easy, evolved.

What I didn't realize was the quiet cost. Every time I adjusted myself to meet someone else's needs, I moved a little further away from my own. My truth, my preferences, and my internal signals were the ones being edited out. Over time, that kind of self-erasure takes a toll on both the mind and the body.

This is how worth beliefs work. They convince you that belonging and safety are conditional.

So you learn to be enough.

- good enough
- easy enough
- useful enough
- calm enough
- agreeable enough
- impressive enough
- low-maintenance enough

Because anything else feels like it risks disconnection. And to the survival brain, disconnection feels like danger.

Reflection

Can I think of a recent moment when I felt the need to prove my worth in order to feel secure?

With a friend? A partner? At work? Or even with myself?

Just notice. This awareness is how these patterns begin to loosen.

____

____

____

____

____

____

3. Power Beliefs: "Do I have any influence here?"

Power beliefs form last. They develop around how your environment responded to your efforts: your voice, your ideas, your boundaries.

If your early attempts at authentic expression were ignored, dismissed, shut down, or punished, your HOS learned a heavy rule:

"My voice doesn't create change. I have no power as my authentic self."

When a child learns this, the body responds by shrinking its influence. This doesn't mean the child is naturally *passive*; it means it feels safer to *sacrifice* their needs and authentic emotions than to risk conflict or rejection.

This shows up later as:

- shutting down emotionally

- avoiding hard conversations
- letting others take the lead
- doubting your own capability
- feeling overwhelmed by normal levels of responsibility
- self-sacrifice or not knowing how to hold boundaries

On the opposite end, some children learn another pattern:

"The only time anyone responds to me is when I escalate."

This teaches the body that intensity is the only effective tool. Not because the child is always "angry," but because escalation was the only strategy that ever worked.

From here, the system may learn:

- "I can't get my needs met when I'm calm or happy."
- "I can't be heard unless I escalate and get louder."
- "Anger is the only influence I have."

This is the root of explosive reactions.

Power beliefs shape whether you move through life with agency or avoidance or anger. All of which stem from the same place: a young nervous system trying to understand whether it mattered.

Reflection

Can I get curious about how I learned to show up in my early years?

Did I adapt by becoming quieter, easier, or conflict-avoiding?

Or did I learn to become louder, more visible, more capable, or more impressive?

Or did I shift between roles depending on the people and environments around me?

(These weren't personality traits. They were strategies for connection.)

____

____

____

____

____

____

The Big Truth About These Three Beliefs

These beliefs weren't created to make you happy. They were created to keep you alive.

That's why they feel so real.

That's why they override mindset.

That's why they outlast logic.

That's why they show up everywhere.

It's also why changing them feels uncomfortable. Your nervous system learned that unfamiliar behaviors might be dangerous, and unless challenged, old beliefs stick — even when you grow out of the zoo.

Seeing these beliefs clearly is the first step in shifting them.

You can't change a belief you can't see.

You can't choose a new belief until you understand the rule it's replacing.

Reflection

Take your time with this.

Which of the three beliefs, safety, worth, or power, shows up most in my life today?

Where do I notice it in my daily life: in my thoughts, my choices, my reactions or the way I relate to people?

How might it be shaping what I reach for, what I avoid, and what I believe is possible for me right now?

____

____

____

____

____

____

Survival Beliefs vs. Aligned Beliefs

Survival beliefs and aligned beliefs can feel similar, but they come from opposite places in the nervous system. One is born from protection; the other is born from presence. One forms in stress; the other forms in calm. One is often inherited; the other is chosen.

A survival belief is a feeling-based rule your younger HOS created to stay attached, accepted and safe. It's fast, automatic and deeply familiar. Your HOS returns to it because it recognizes it. Even when it hurts, it feels like home.

An aligned belief works differently. It's chosen in the present with a regulated HOS, shaped by clarity, agency, and the identity you're consciously building rather than the identity you learned to perform as a child. Aligned beliefs move more slowly. They feel steadier, and at first, they require regulation to access because your system hasn't practiced them yet.

This distinction matters because your HOS chooses what feels safe, not what's true. To the brain, safe simply means predictable.

That's why familiar pain often wins over unfamiliar possibility. The system trusts what it has repeated, even when it costs you connection, confidence or ease.

You can see this in perception itself. To return to our earlier metaphor, survival beliefs act like sunglasses with tiny holes poked in them. You notice the moments that confirm the rule and overlook the many that contradict it. Your HOS edits experience to protect what it already knows.

You can logically know *I am safe* and still feel abandoned when a message goes unanswered. You can intellectually believe *I am enough* and still feel unworthy when someone sounds disappointed.

The survival belief fires first, and perception organizes around it before reasoning has time to respond.

Aligned beliefs require a different internal state, especially in the beginning. They require enough calm for the nervous system to update its predictions. Enough calm for the brain to consider something new. Enough calm for you to choose a belief that supports who you're becoming, rather than one that once protected who you had to be.

When aligned beliefs begin to take root, they don't feel *true* at first. They feel unfamiliar and uncertain. They feel like stepping into a room you've never been in before. Like catching a glimpse of a life you've never allowed yourself to imagine, or perhaps like standing at the edge of the zoo you grew up in and suddenly seeing the wide open world beyond the walls.

It can feel scary, because unfamiliarity always does. But it's also electric. These beliefs carry a spark of possibility your system hasn't yet practiced. They feel like a horizon calling you forward, even while the old instinct in you wants to stay where things are known, predictable and safe enough.

But unfamiliar doesn't mean unsafe. It simply means unpracticed.

This is where belief transformation begins. As you become more aware of your beliefs, you give your system the chance to experience a new emotional pattern long enough for the belief beneath it to become the new familiar. Awareness isn't just insight, it's the start of a new way of being, creating the moments your nervous system needs to begin rewriting old rules into something that supports your evolution.

And once that process begins, aligned beliefs start to feel as natural as survival beliefs once did.

Reflection

Where in my life do I feel like I cling to familiar patterns even when they limit me or feel uncomfortable?

Which aligned belief feels true in my mind but not yet safe in my body?

____

____

____

____

____

____

How Beliefs Shape Behavior

Your behavior isn't mysterious. It isn't random. And it's rarely about willpower. Most behavior is simply the physical expression of the beliefs you carry — especially the old, practiced beliefs.

If your core belief says, *"I need to keep everyone happy to stay safe,"* you'll move toward people pleasing without thinking. If your belief says, *"I must stay alert,"* you'll double-check everything, anticipate problems, and struggle to rest even when you want to. If your belief says, *"I have to earn love,"* you'll work harder than everyone else, still feel like it isn't enough, and start to feel bitter that others aren't trying as hard.

You aren't choosing these behaviors in the moment. The belief is choosing for you.

Beliefs shape:

- how quickly you say yes

- how often you apologize
- whether you take risks
- whether you speak up
- how you handle conflict
- whether you avoid hard conversations
- how you show up at work, in love, in parenting and even in your health

Some examples in everyday life may look like:

If a belief says, *"Conflict is dangerous,"* then your body will shut down or become flooded when tension rises, even if your mindset says, *"I want to communicate well."*

If a belief says, *"Mistakes are unacceptable,"* then you'll procrastinate or overprepare because your HOS has learned that hesitation feels safer than being wrong.

And if a belief says, *"I'm not valuable unless I perform,"* then every behavior in your life will bend around proving your worth, even at the cost of your health.

Behavior is the visible layer.

Belief is the architecture beneath it.

And until you understand the architecture, the same behaviors will keep rebuilding themselves.

This is why behavior change so often fails. We try to remodel the house without ever examining the foundation. We repaint the walls, move the furniture, rearrange the habits... but the structure underneath hasn't changed. The old blueprint is still running the show.

To create lasting change, you don't start with the behavior. You start with the belief that built it.

Because once you see the belief, *truly* see it, you can shift. Your behavior becomes easier to change because you're no longer fighting yourself. You're updating the operating system instead of wrestling with the output.

We'll go much deeper into behavior in future chapters, but for now, your only job is to notice the connection: your actions make perfect sense when you remember the belief that shaped them.

Reflection

What is one behavior I am struggling with that suddenly makes sense when I consider the belief underneath it? (for example: exercise, paying bills, replying to texts)

Where did that belief come from?

And what behavior might be possible if a different belief were running the show?

____

____

____

____

____

____

The Personal Power Practice: Raising Awareness

Belief change begins with awareness. Not heroic discipline. Not a perfect mindset. Awareness.

Most people imagine beliefs living deep in the subconscious, far removed from daily life. In reality, they surface in small, ordinary moments. The eye roll and irritation before you reply. The immediate feeling of nausea when you see an old friend. The holding of your breath when the phone rings.

Beliefs rarely arrive as sentences. They arrive as sensations. When you catch them early, before they take over, you access something that feels like real personal power.

This practice has a single purpose: to give you a moment of clarity before an old belief becomes the lens you see through. In that pause, choice becomes possible.

Tool: The Belief-Catching Practice

When you notice a strong reaction to your circumstances, ask yourself:

What belief might be running right now?

Is this a Survival belief or an Aligned belief?

How does believing this help me right now?

Survival beliefs formed to protect you.

Aligned beliefs support the life you're consciously building.

You don't need to change anything in that moment. You only need to notice which belief is guiding you.

Because once a belief becomes visible, it stops acting like truth and becomes something you can work with.

Beliefs rarely appear as clear thoughts you can easily examine. Most of the time, they show up much earlier through a tightening in the body, a sudden shift in mood or an emotion that seems to arrive out of nowhere. That's because emotions are often the first signal that a belief has been activated.

Understanding this invisible link between belief and emotion is the next step in learning how your Human Operating System works.

Chapter 5
The Invisible Link Between Beliefs and Emotion

Feelings aren't reactions to life, but reactions to meaning.

In this chapter, we'll explore why emotions don't come from situations themselves, but from the beliefs your nervous system uses to interpret them. You'll see how feelings reveal the internal rules shaping your reactions, why emotions repeat even when you "know better," and how calm creates the conditions for emotional patterns to complete rather than recycle.

Most people assume their emotions come directly from the situations in front of them. A tone, a silence, a delay, a raised eyebrow, a forgotten message, each one can spark a wave of feeling before we can consciously figure out why. It feels natural to blame the moment. It feels natural to say, *"You hurt my feelings,"* or *"That made me anxious,"* or *"This situation overwhelmed me."*

But emotions don't arise from the situation itself. They arise from the meaning your HOS assigns to the moment, and that meaning comes from the beliefs you carry.

Your emotions reflect the rules your system has practiced for years. They aren't random. They're familiar. They reveal what your HOS expects, what it remembers, and what it believes will keep you safe. This is why two people can sit in the same room and have completely different emotional experiences. They aren't reacting to the room.

They're reacting to the beliefs that interpret the room.

Your Emotions Are the Body Recognizing a Pattern

As we now know, the body reacts before the mind. It listens for patterns, not explanations. When something in the present echoes something from your past, your body prepares for the meaning it learned to expect. This happens faster than thought. It happens through sensation, and it happens in service of protection.

This is why a criticism can feel like rejection, why a small mistake can trigger anxiety, and why a tense silence can feel like danger or punishment. Your emotional response isn't reacting only to the moment itself. It's reacting to the belief and emotional pattern the moment awakens.

The science behind this is deeply human. The brain survives through prediction. When a current experience resembles an old emotional pattern, the body reacts instantly, before logic has time to weigh in. This is why emotions so often feel bigger than the situation at hand. You aren't just feeling the present.

You're feeling the past inside the present.

This is what emotions truly are. They aren't flaws or failures. **Emotions are messages from the beliefs your system uses to navigate the world.** They reveal which internal rule has been activated. They show you what your body is still trying to protect. They point to the story your HOS still believes is true.

Often, emotions rise not to overwhelm you, but because something in you is ready to be seen, processed and released. When you stay with the feeling of an emotion instead of reacting right away, you give your body the space to update the cause of the emotion. In that space, emotions stop feeling like something to control or suppress. They become information, clear, honest and human.

Here's why.

At a physiological level, **emotions are energy moving through the body**. When your nervous system assigns meaning to a moment, it mobilizes energy to respond. That energy creates sensation, heat, tension, impulse and movement. In a regulated body, the energy rises, completes its purpose, and then settles. This is how the nervous system returns to balance.

You can see this clearly in animals. A deer freezes when threatened, then shakes once the danger has passed. A dog growls, runs, discharges and returns to rest. Their bodies complete the cycle. Nothing is stored. Nothing lingers.

Unfortunately, in their youth, most humans learn to interrupt this process. We're taught to suppress emotion, explain it away, override it with logic, or turn it into behavior before it finishes moving. We tighten our jaw, hold our breath, distract ourselves, or tell ourselves to calm down and push forward.

When emotional energy is interrupted instead of completed, it doesn't disappear. It remains stored in the nervous system as unfinished activation. Over time, this deepens emotional patterns. Reactions arrive faster. Triggers feel sharper. The same feelings repeat because the system never received the signal that the experience ended and safety returned. In simpler words, the emotional energy is still stuck.

This is why suppressed emotions often come back louder rather than quieter. The body isn't trying to overwhelm you. It's trying to finish something it was never allowed to complete.

When an emotion rises and is immediately shut down (suppressed), the belief beneath it stays intact. The nervous system never updates its prediction. Instead, it learns that the feeling itself is dangerous or uncomfortable, which reinforces the very belief the emotion was pointing to in the first place.

Allowing an emotion to move through the body with awareness and calm is what allows it to resolve. Not reliving the story. Not analyzing it endlessly. Not acting it out. Simply staying present and experiencing the physical, emotional sensation as it rises, peaks, and softens.

One way to imagine this is like light passing through glass. The light interacts with the glass briefly, but it ultimately moves through to the other side. In the same way, an emotion can move through your body. You feel the sensations it creates, stay present with them, and allow the experience to pass instead of stopping it.

This is how old survival beliefs begin to loosen and strong emotions begin to fade. Not through force, but through completion. When emotions are allowed to move, they stop needing to repeat themselves through behavior.

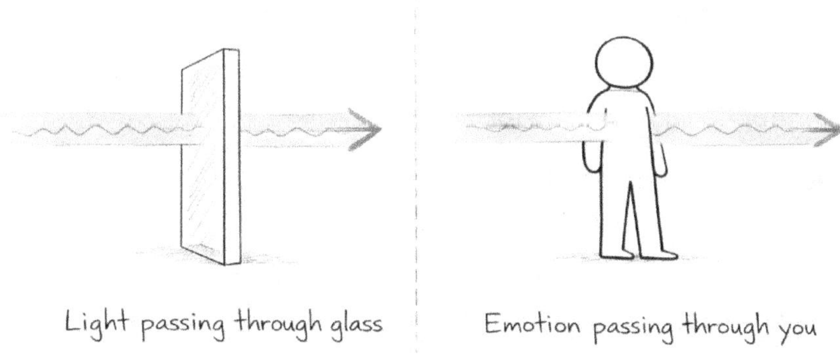

The system learns that uncomfortable emotions do not always equal danger, and calm can become associated with presence and choice rather than withdrawal or disconnection.

Emotion, when met this way, becomes information instead of interruption.

When you begin to understand emotions this way, their meaning becomes easier to interpret. Anger often arises when a belief about boundaries, respect or competence is touched. Sadness appears when a belief about connection or belonging is activated. Anxiety shows up when a belief about safety or preparedness is stirred. Shame surfaces when a belief about worth is threatened.

These emotions may feel sudden, but they aren't sudden to your system. They're familiar pathways traveled many times before. The body isn't overreacting. It's remembering the emotional meaning it learned long ago to keep you safe.

This is why mindset alone can't override emotion. The body responds first and the mind more slowly, even if we're talking microseconds. Logic can't soothe a belief that lives beneath thought. Only awareness, paired with calm, can begin to change it.

The Meaning Behind Different Emotions

When you understand that emotions reflect beliefs, they become easier to interpret rather than something to manage or suppress.

Anger often rises when a belief about boundaries, respect or competence is touched. It signals that something feels crossed or violated.

Sadness appears when a belief about connection or belonging is activated. It reflects loss, distance, or the fear that something meaningful may be slipping away.

Anxiety arrives when a belief about safety, preparedness, or uncertainty is stirred. It's the HOS scanning ahead, trying to predict and prevent harm.

Shame surfaces when a belief about worth is threatened. It carries the fear of being exposed, judged, or found lacking.

Guilt often emerges when a belief about responsibility or moral alignment is activated. It reflects concern about having caused harm or violated an internal rule.

Frustration shows up when a belief about control or progress is blocked. It's the tension between effort and outcome.

Bitterness develops when a belief about fairness or reciprocity has been violated repeatedly. It forms when giving goes unseen for too long and hope quietly turns into self-protection.

Understanding Emotions Is the Doorway to Change

Once you understand that emotions rise from beliefs, every reaction becomes information.

Instead of asking, *"Why am I feeling this way?"* you begin asking, *"What belief is attached to this emotion?"*

That single shift opens up the possibility for real change.

It changes how you move through relationships, how you communicate, how you navigate conflict, how you relate to your own worth and how you set boundaries. It shapes how you show up as a parent, a partner, a leader and a human being. Most importantly, it restores your ability to choose your response instead of being pulled by patterns that formed before you had a voice.

Emotion is not the enemy of change.

Emotion is the doorway.

It points you toward the belief beneath the reaction. And once that belief becomes visible, it can be met with awareness instead of resistance. From there, change no longer requires force. It unfolds gently, safely, and with a depth that mindset alone could never reach.

In the next section, we explore why these beliefs feel so convincing, even when they no longer match your life, and why the nervous system is wired to prefer the familiar over the true.

Reflection

Which emotion arrives the fastest for me?

And what early emotional rule(s) might still be shaping that response today?

____

____

____

____

____

____

Noticing Old Belief and Emotion Pairs

One of the most common belief and emotion pairs I see, in my clients and in myself, is the quiet conviction that when things are going too well, something must be about to go wrong.

It sounds practical. Even responsible. Beneath it, though, lives a survival rule that says steady, easy moments are suspicious, joy is fragile, and calm never lasts.

For years, I didn't question this pattern. When life felt easy — a peaceful morning, a slow afternoon, a day without urgency — a small wave of anxiety would rise. A tightening across my shoulders. A sense of raised alertness. Suspicion and worry.

Nothing had happened, yet my body responded as if something had. The survival belief arrived so quickly it felt like intuition rather than pattern. That's how beliefs often work.

They disguise themselves as emotional truth.

"Waiting for the Other Shoe to Drop" and Catching the Pattern Before It Takes Over

It showed up one quiet afternoon while I was folding laundry. Sunlight streamed through the window. Nothing demanded anything from me.

And then it happened.

A faint ripple of unease paired with an intense tightening beneath my ribs — the familiar whisper that life had become too quiet and easy, which meant something was coming.

For most of my life, that feeling would have carried me away. I would have followed it into scanning, replaying, worrying, trying to locate the problem my body insisted must exist.

This time, however, I paused.

I softened my posture. I took one slow breath. I rolled my shoulders and slowly scanned the room — all signals to my body that it was safe to relax. Just enough calm to steady myself.

And then a new question had space to surface:

Is something actually wrong, or is this the belief that easy is unsafe?

The answer came quickly. Nothing was wrong. Nothing needed my fear. The sensation wasn't a warning. It was a body memory, an old belief resurfacing out of habit, trying to protect me the only way it knew how: by predicting a problem.

The power of that moment was that once I recognized what was happening — my body reacting to an old belief — I was able to stay with the anxiety in my body without needing to create a story around it.

Even though the anxious feeling didn't disappear instantly, old patterns rarely do — the belief loosened its grip on my body and my mind.

I felt myself return to the present. And in that return, something shifted inside me.

Calm and curiosity gave me my power back — not just over how my body felt, but over my thoughts as well.

That moment is the heart of personal power: recognizing the belief inside the emotion before it becomes your reality. Choosing the present over prediction. Staying with yourself long enough to step out of a story that no longer fits.

Tool: A Somatic Check-In to Gain Clarity and Release Old Belief and Emotion Pairs

You don't need a journal or a long ritual. You need a moment of noticing and curiosity.

The goal of this practice is simple: to let the emotion move through, and to notice whether a belief is present without trying to solve it.

This isn't belief work. This is emotional completion and information gathering.

Here's the rhythm:

First, notice the initial signal.
This is the earliest moment something shifts. A tightening in the face, shoulders or stomach. A change in breath. A wave of emotion. A quick, uncomfortable thought. This is the moment before the reaction gains momentum, when awareness still has room.

Next, feel what's happening in your body.
Not the story. Not the explanation. Just the sensation itself. Stay with it as sensation rather than meaning. Many emotions are unfinished experiences looking for completion, and the body releases them far more efficiently when they are met with acknowledgement rather than analysis.

Then, notice what it seems connected to, if anything.

Sometimes a belief becomes obvious, like calm is unsafe or I always mess things up. Sometimes there's no clear belief at all, only activation. Both are completely valid. You aren't required to name or fix anything here. You're simply noticing what shows up.

Ask gently, "Is this now, or is this then?"
This question creates space. It helps you sense whether your body is responding to the present moment or to an old emotional memory surfacing to be released. Many reactions aren't warnings. They're echoes.

Allow the emotion to complete.
Instead of suppressing or distracting, let the sensation rise, peak and soften. This teaches your HOS that it's safe to feel without needing to act or control. When emotions are allowed to finish, they lose their energy.

Finally, choose your next step from calm.
Once the body settles even a little, clarity returns. You can sense whether action is actually needed, a boundary, a conversation, a pause, or whether nothing needs to be done at all because the emotion has already passed.

If a belief surfaces and continues to repeat, that's information you can work with later.

If nothing lingered, the emotion simply needed completion.

The purpose of this is to listen long enough to know what, if anything, requires attention and start gathering data about what's happening in your HOS.

Why Somatic Sensing and Belief Catching Works

Each time you catch a belief while it's still forming, something subtly shifts. The old pattern loses a bit of authority, and a small window of choice opens. You begin to feel the difference between living from memory and living from the present moment.

The change is sometimes hard to notice. It doesn't arrive with fireworks. It shows up in the space after you've been consistent with this process. It may feel like daily ease or satisfaction, or the simple realization that you have more room and control inside than you thought.

With repetition, calm becomes familiar. Your nervous system starts to expect safety and growth rather than threat. **Your beliefs begin reflecting where you are headed instead of where you came from.**

Real change rarely announces itself. It accumulates. It builds quietly. It begins in these small moments where awareness replaces outdated instinct and presence replaces prediction.

Over time, those moments begin to shape how you live.

Reflection

Where in my life am I starting to notice a little more space between my initial emotional reaction and how I respond?

____

____

____

____

____

____

The Power of Visualization to Shift Old Beliefs

There's another way your system can begin to update old belief and emotion patterns before the real moment even happens: visualization.

Your brain doesn't fully separate imagination from real experience. When you vividly picture an event, your body begins to respond as if it's happening. Your heart rate can shift. Your muscles subtly prepare. Emotions begin to rise. The nervous system starts running the pattern.

This is why athletes, performers, surgeons, executives, and pilots mentally rehearse before important moments. They aren't just thinking about success. They're training their nervous system to recognize the situation ahead of time.

When you pair visualization with body awareness and regulation, something powerful happens.

Your HOS activates as if the moment is real, and instead of getting pulled into the reaction, you stay with your body and guide it back to calm.

The brain begins to learn a new association: this situation can happen, and I can stay steady inside it.

Over time, the prediction changes.

The body begins to expect calm and confidence instead of threat.

Tool: Rehearsing Safety

Think of a moment that usually creates a reaction in you.

A conversation. A presentation. A pause in a relationship. Something real.

Close your eyes and picture the moment as if it's happening right now.

Let it feel real enough that your body responds.

Notice what shows up.

Tightness. Breath-holding. Emotion rising.

Now stay with both:

the imagined moment…

and the feelings you are experiencing in your body.

Keep the scene in your mind while you gently regulate your body.

Soften your shoulders. Take a slow breath out.

Let your body feel the emotion and settle at the same time.

You're not trying to remove the feeling.

You're showing your system that the feeling can move through you ... and you're still safe.

Stay there for a few breaths.

Then come back to the present moment.

Repeat this a few times.

Each time, your body learns something new: *I can feel this... and remain steady and present.*

I can be in this situation... and still be assured of myself.

With this tool, visualization introduces the experience. Feeling the emotion allows the pattern to complete. Calm begins to rewrite the belief.

Calm Paves the Way to a New Belief

Calm doesn't mean negative emotions disappear. It means you have access to yourself while these emotions are present, and you can create new belief patterns.

This is why understanding emotions matters. They show you the active belief... and give you a chance to meet it differently. You don't need to argue with an old belief. You can give your body a new experience to change it. Because beliefs don't change all at once, they shift through experience.

With repetition, the old rules loosen, and new ones begin to take their place. You are no longer living inside a story written in the past. You are beginning to choose the one you live now.

Reflection

What parts of my life does my body still brace for an outcome that belongs to my past rather than my present?

When an emotion rises, can I pause long enough to notice what my body is feeling... and what belief might be guiding it before I respond?

____

____

____

____

____

____

A Note for Those Wanting Faster Change

You may find yourself wanting a more direct technique for belief change. That impulse is natural and makes sense. When something hurts, it's human to want it to shift quickly.

What matters most is *when* and *how* belief work is introduced.

Beliefs change fastest when the body can stay regulated while a new experience is happening. Without that foundation, even the most effective techniques tend to work temporarily or collapse under stress. With it, however, belief change becomes sustainable.

The tools in this book are designed to build the foundation first. More targeted belief work belongs later in the transformation process, once your HOS has the capacity to hold it without slipping back into protection. Refer to the Mindset section in the next chapter to rewire the belief.

Before we move forward, it's important to understand what becomes possible when you begin living this way. When you learn how to calm your body, notice old beliefs as they activate, and return to the present moment, you restore a capacity that many people slowly lose under stress: the ability to think clearly.

This isn't about positive thinking or mental discipline. It's about creating enough internal safety for your mind to interpret what's actually happening in front of you, rather than reacting through the emotional predictions of the past.

When the body settles, the mind finally has space to participate. It can organize insight, make meaning from experience, imagine new possibilities, and choose responses that support the identity you're stepping into.

From this state, your mindset becomes easier to work with and easier to trust.

Chapter 6
How to Unlock the Power of Mindset

Mindset becomes powerful only when your nervous system feels safe enough to let your mind lead instead of react.

This chapter explains why mindset tools work sometimes — and completely fall apart other times. You'll learn how chronic stress quietly keeps your brain in protection mode, why awareness and curiosity restore choice, and how emotions and body signals become essential information instead of obstacles.

Through practical tools like the Research Scientist mindset and the FLOW Set Point, this chapter shows you how to calm the body first and widen perception. From there, thinking becomes a strategic partner to your nervous system — so mindset supports clarity, direction, and aligned action rather than becoming another form of self-pressure.

Why Mindset Tools Only Work Some of the Time

We often believe mindset works because we assume we control our thoughts. If we think better, we live better. But the brain isn't only thinking. It's constantly reading information from the rest of the system.

At every moment, the brain receives signals from the body, compares them to past experiences and beliefs, interprets what's happening, and decides how to respond. Because this is far more information than conscious awareness can manage, the brain moves many processes to autopilot. Habits, reactions, emotional tendencies, and familiar behaviors run automatically so attention can focus on the present moment. Under normal conditions, this works well and allows life to feel manageable.

The difficulty begins when the body feels under pressure. When the nervous system senses threat, the brain shifts priorities. Instead of reflecting, imagining, or choosing carefully, it begins trying to resolve the signals coming from the body. Attention narrows, creativity decreases and familiar reactions take over. The brain isn't failing in these moments — it's occupied.

When stress has been present for long periods, much of the mind's capacity is spent monitoring internal alarms. In that state, trying to change thoughts alone is difficult because attention keeps being pulled toward perceived danger. Lasting change rarely begins with thinking differently. The body must first become quiet enough that the mind has space to lead.

Imagine this as a house filled with fire alarms. When alarms are blaring, the mind moves from room to room searching for the source. It can't settle in the room it's actually in. As the nervous system regulates, the alarms quiet. Only then can attention return to the present moment and choice becomes available again.

Reflection

Where in my life do I understand what I want to change, yet notice my body responding from urgency, habit or protection?

When stress shows up for me, what do my "internal alarms" usually sound like (thoughts, sensations, emotions)?

____

____

____

____

____

____

From Autopilot to Choice

This is where things start to get interesting.

Regulation does more than help you feel better. It restores awareness. Instead of being pulled forward by urgency, habit, or reflex, you regain the ability to notice what's actually happening inside you and around you. You begin responding rather than reacting. And curiosity becomes a powerful tool.

When the body is under stress, the mind searches for certainty. It wants quick answers, familiar conclusions and predictable outcomes. When the body settles, the mind can ask better questions. It can pause long enough to recognize whether a thought belongs to the present moment or to an old pattern repeating itself, and whether you want to keep following it.

Earlier, we described beliefs as filters shaped by past experience. Under pressure, those filters automatically slide into place. Thoughts feel true even when they're simply familiar. Assumptions learned long ago quietly organize perception without your awareness.

With enough internal calm, you can finally see the filter instead of looking through it.

Mindset now becomes useful in a different way. Not as a tool to force change, but as a way to observe patterns, question them, and gradually choose what fits the person you're becoming. You're no longer trying to override emotion the moment it appears. You're creating the conditions that allow clear choice to exist at all.

This is the beginning of living aligned with your mind instead of being managed by old reactions. You're standing at the trailhead of a deliberate life.

Reflection

What does autopilot look like for me on a normal day, especially under pressure?

Remember, awareness leads to choice.

____

____

____

____

____

____

The Wiser Mind Superpower #1: Becoming the Research Scientist of Your Life

When the alarms quiet, the mind stops racing around trying to fix, predict, or prevent, and begins to notice instead. Now the Wiser mind kicks on, and mindset becomes a useful tool for increased self-understanding and a guide for creating your desired future.

Most of the time, we aren't thinking *about* our thoughts. We're inside them. They arrive fully formed, feel convincing, and carry us into action before we realize what has happened. Once autopilot is turned off, we have an opportunity to start seeing our thoughts instead of being stuck living from them.

When I work with clients, I have them pretend to be the Research Scientist for their own mind and body. A scientist who is not there to judge, fix, or analyze in the moment, but instead a curious observer — present and available to witness.

Imagine yourself moving through your life with a clipboard and pen, curious and attentive, simply noticing and taking notes about what unfolds. No labels or judgements. **Just data.**

A thought or belief appears. *Hmm. That's interesting.*

A familiar emotional reaction returns. *Hmm. That pattern again.*

A behavior repeats. *Hmm. I wonder why I do that?*

This tool is effective because curiosity replaces self-criticism, and neutral observation — along with grace — replaces shame. Life becomes something you can work with **instead of something that keeps happening to you.**

This is the return of agency and choice.

Once you can see a thought, you can choose how to relate to it. Once you can recognize a pattern, you can begin choosing a new one. Once you can observe a belief without immediately acting from it, you gain access to the question that creates true alignment:

Is that what I believe now?

Opportunity abounds when you're back in the driver's seat, taking in data and deciding what to do with it.

Reflection

What is one recurring thought I've noticed lately that I can simply observe instead of judge? And where do I feel it in my body?

If I approached my inner world with curiosity instead of criticism, what might I learn?

Curiosity changes your relationship to what you find there.

____

____

____

____

____

____

The Wiser Mind Superpower #2: Using Awareness to Strategize Stress

In this moment of newfound awareness, it can be tempting to immediately start planning outcomes like getting the promotion, finding a partner, improving your health, or fixing your life. But before any of that can take place, there's a more essential question the Wiser mind needs to ask:

How do I keep my HOS regulated enough (physically and emotionally) to make conscious choices?

This is where mindset begins to do its most important work. Not by ignoring stress or pushing through it, but by *strategizing* stress.

Stress is not the enemy. It's information. The body is constantly communicating through tension, fatigue, emotion, irritation, restlessness, shutdown and overwhelm. These signals aren't flaws to overcome — they're guidance, letting you know when your body needs support, when you're approaching your limits, or when you're pushing beyond what is sustainable.

Mindset's core job is to learn how to listen to this information and respond intelligently.

The mind can partner with the body to make strategic choices that protect stability. As you practice greater self-awareness, you begin to notice what truly supports regulation and what quietly erodes it. Certain environments, conversations, work rhythms, foods, sleep patterns, and expectations either help your HOS stay balanced or slowly push it toward overload. When awareness is present, these patterns become easier to recognize.

This is the true beginning of intentional behavior. You're no longer reacting after the fact. You're using the body's signals as early indicators, adjusting before stress turns into burnout, illness, or emotional reactivity.

Over time, this becomes a way of living rather than a technique. Just like fostering a new habit, you begin pacing yourself differently. You build in nervous system regulators before things fall apart. You recognize when to rest, when to move, when to connect, and when to pull back. The goal isn't to eliminate stress, but to work with it skillfully and strategically so it doesn't accumulate faster than your HOS can release it.

These actions aren't coping mechanisms. They're conscious **regulation strategies**, and they form the foundation of sustainable performance, emotional health and long-term wellbeing.

When calm stops feeling like something that randomly appears and starts becoming something you know how to maintain, mindset has found its rightful role as a strategic partner to the body, helping you stay regulated enough to think clearly, choose wisely and live in alignment.

Reflection

What signals does my body give me when I'm approaching overload?

(This may be the most important question you can ask. Stress is information. Awareness turns it into strategy.)

Which environments, rhythms, or expectations genuinely support my regulation, and which drain it?

____

____

____

____

____

____

Mindset's Missing Link: Emotional Awareness as Information

Up to this point, mindset has been framed primarily as a tool for understanding thoughts, beliefs and body alarms. But there's another layer of awareness that's just as essential and often overlooked: emotions.

Emotions aren't separate from the nervous system. They're the nervous system's *felt language*. Sensations in the body tell you **where** stress is held. Emotions tell you **how** your HOS is interpreting what's happening.

When mindset expands to include emotional awareness, it becomes far more effective.

Instead of asking only, *What am I thinking?* you begin asking:

What am I feeling?

What is my body responding to and why?

What state am I operating from right now?

This matters because emotions influence thoughts far more frequently than thoughts influence emotions. When the body is activated, the mind will generate thoughts that match that emotional state. Fear produces fearful thinking (e.g., anxiety and worry). Anger produces the search for external circumstances you can blame. Sadness produces thoughts around poor self-worth, loss and lack. Trying to "think positive" from these states often fails because the emotional environment isn't supportive yet.

This is why emotional awareness isn't a detour from mindset work. It's the key piece to be aware of.

When you can detect emotional signals early, irritation, frustration, restlessness, sadness, worry, you gain valuable information about what your HOS needs before those emotions grab hold as stories, reactions, or decisions. Emotions become data, not directives.

Mindset's role here is simple but powerful: to notice emotional state, respond with regulation, and then choose the next step with grace and intention.

This is where choice truly becomes available. And while it may sound impossible at first, you do have influence over how you feel not by forcing new emotion, but by knowing how to guide your HOS toward a more supportive, better feeling state.

Enter stage left... FLOW Set Point.

Reflection

When emotions arise, do I tend to treat them as messages or as problems to eliminate?

____

____

____

____

____

____

Tool: FLOW Set Point (the most powerful tool in this book)

The FLOW Set Point is a simple, body-first sequence you can use in real time to regain clarity, choice and direction. It isn't about forcing calm or fixing your thoughts, but rather helping your nervous system settle enough for your Wiser mind to come back online.

Use FLOW anytime you feel rushed, reactive, overwhelmed, foggy, or off-center. Its purpose is practical and immediate: restore enough regulation so you can choose your next step intentionally instead of reacting from habit or stress.

FLOW doesn't eliminate emotion. It gives you access to yourself while emotion is present.

F — Focus and Feel

Begin by paying attention to the body.

Instead of asking, *What's wrong?* or *What should I do?,* bring your awareness to your body.

Where do you feel activation right now?

Tightness? Pressure? Heaviness? Heat? Restlessness? Emotions?

You aren't analyzing. You're locating.

This step shifts you out of mental spin and into the present moment, where change actually happens.

L — Listen and Learn from sensation and emotion

Next, listen without fixing.

Let the sensations and emotions be exactly as they are.

Discomfort, irritation, sadness, fatigue or tension aren't problems to solve — they're signals.

You don't need to explain them or attach a story. Simply acknowledge what's present.

Listening tells the nervous system it has been heard, which often softens the internal alarm on its own.

O — Orient and Open through regulation

Next, help your system reorient to now.

Use a simple regulating cue:

- a longer exhale
- gentle movement
- grounding through your feet
- hands to heart or ribs
- orienting your eyes to the room

In more emotional moments, this may mean staying with the feeling long enough for it to release, without searching for meaning or belief.

The goal is not perfect calm.

The goal is enough regulation to remind the body*: there is no immediate threat right now.*

This is the bridge between body and mind. Choosing to orient and calm the body in the moment will also allow you to open the door (or window) to more internal information, as well as see the external world with more clarity.

W — Witness and Wonder

From this steadier place, witness the moment and what's really happening.

Thoughts may still be present, but now you're observing them rather than believing them automatically. You notice what your mind is saying without arguing, correcting, or following it. Just get curious about them.

Perspective returns here. You can see the aspects of the situation more accurately now.

You're no longer inside the reaction.

You're observing it.

(Some people find it helpful to imagine a bird's-eye view — as if you're gently watching the moment instead of being pulled into it.)

Set Point — Set your next aligned action

Only now do you choose what comes next.

Not the whole day.

Not the whole solution.

Just the next aligned step.

This might be:

- a boundary
- a conversation
- a task

- rest
- movement
- or choosing a belief or intention that fits the present moment

The Set Point keeps choice grounded and manageable, so the nervous system doesn't become overwhelmed again.

FLOW is about building self-awareness.

It's about knowing how to return to center — again and again — and taking agency in the moment.

Each return compounds. Small moments of regulation lead to clearer decisions, steadier behavior and a life that feels more intentional over time.

From Regulation to Action: Where Change Becomes Visible

Up to this point, the work has been internal.

You've learned how your body signals safety and threat, how beliefs shape perception, how emotions carry information and how to return to center using FLOW. This is the foundation. Without it, behavior change collapses under pressure.

But regulation alone isn't the goal.

The real question is what happens **after** you settle.

How you speak.

What you choose.

What you avoid.

What you repeat.

What you change.

This is where behavior enters.

Behavior isn't really about willpower or self-control like we were all raised to believe. It's the visible expression of your internal state. When the nervous system is dysregulated, behavior becomes reactive, patterned and familiar. When the nervous system is regulated, behavior becomes intentional, flexible and aligned.

This is why so many people "know what to do" but struggle to do it. They try to change behavior from the top down, without changing the state that drives it. The result is effort without sustainability.

When you can return to center and calm using FLOW and other regulation tools, you take back your power.

You can pause between impulse and action. You actually gain access to choice, and you start to respond instead of react.

Behavior is what you do with that pause.

It's not about forcing yourself to be different. It's about allowing your actions to reflect the version of you that's finally understood and supported from within.

This is where internal work becomes visible — where alignment, peace, and authenticity begin to show up in how you live.

Chapter 7
Behavior Is the End of the HOS Chain

Behavior is the final output of your Human Operating System — a reflection of your internal state, not your identity.

This chapter shows why behavior change so often feels frustrating, even when you "know better." You'll learn how stress states create state-dependent reactions (like snapping, shutting down, avoiding or freezing), why the brain defaults to what's familiar under pressure, and how procrastination is often protection rather than laziness.

You'll also learn practical ways to create space before a reaction takes over — including "Asking Your HOS Why," the Marble Jar capacity model, and the "Feel It to Heal It" reset. These tools help your body process what it's been holding so you can come back to choice and respond in a way that feels more like you.

Most people believe their behavior reveals who they are — their discipline, their strength, their flaws, their character.

But behavior is almost never the starting point. It's the ending point. The final output of a system that has already been practicing a way of BE-ing for years.

In the Human Operating System, behavior is the part of the house others can see. It's how you move through your day, how you speak under pressure, how you react, withdraw, engage, or avoid. Remember, if your HOS was an ant farm, behavior would be the only thing people would be paying attention to from the outside. They would watch your movements and assume they understand the whole structure — or simply that they understand you.

But behavior is never the whole house.

What's visible is activity, not the internal foundation. Motion and emotion, not meaning. Behavior reflects how safe or strained it feels to live inside your internal world, not who you are at your core. When the foundation is firm, behavior looks intentional and aligned. When the foundation is overwhelmed, cracked, or carrying more pressure than it can hold, behavior looks reactive, guarded, or exhausting.

Behavior isn't the problem to fix. (I know that may be hard to believe.)

It's the signal pointing you back to the systems driving it.

In the Human Operating System, behavior happens last.

Reading Behavior
Through Calm and Curiosity

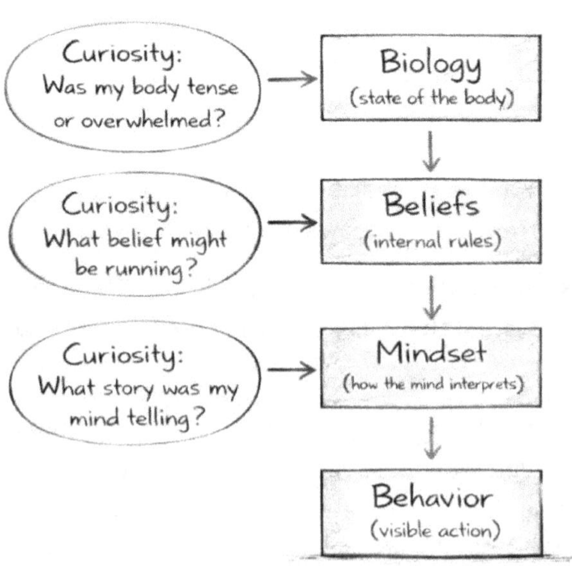

Behavior is the end of the chain.

Calm gives you space to find the cause.

Biology sets the state.

Beliefs interpret the state.

Mindset works with what's available.

Behavior becomes the result.

There's a reason neuroscience calls this **state-dependent behavior**. Your body sets the state, and that state primes your thoughts, impulses, reactions, tone of voice, patience and choices. Biology fires first, and psychology follows its lead.

As you know by now, when your HOS is calm, the thinking brain comes online. You remember your values. You can pause, reflect, choose. You respond like the version of yourself you admire, the one you keep trying to become — and that's the goal.

This is what most people don't understand, though: **your behavior isn't a mystery. It's a reflection of your biology and thoughts.**

It reflects the internal state you're in, not the person you're failing to be.

A regulated nervous system gives you the chance to ask yourself this powerful question:

"Who do I want to be in this moment?"

Reflection

Where in my life do I judge myself (or feel judged) based on behavior?

Have I ever noticed the state of my biology or the beliefs associated with that behavior?

____

____

____

____

____

____

Why You Do Things You *Don't* Want to Do

I worked with a man who told me he felt "possessed" during certain moments of stress. Not metaphorically, truly overtaken. He was gentle, thoughtful, and self-aware, the kind of person who apologized for things that weren't his fault. And yet under pressure, he transformed into someone sharp and easily provoked.

Every morning, he made the same quiet promise to himself: *Today will be different.* And he meant it.

He wasn't lying or avoiding the work. He believed in that promise completely. But somewhere between his morning coffee and the afternoon meeting, a small disruption would land — a missed email, a strained tone, a delay — and without warning, he was gone. The man who made the promise was replaced by a version of himself he barely recognized.

“It’s like my mouth moves before I even know I’m angry,” he said once. “I’m watching myself do it, and I still can’t stop.”

He wasn’t exaggerating. He was describing biology.

What he experienced is often called **limbic hijack**. The emotional centers of the brain fire in milliseconds. The reflective, reasoning part of the brain takes longer to engage. By the time conscious awareness arrives, the body has already chosen a direction. Muscles have tightened. Breath has shifted. Stress hormones are circulating.

This is why your voice snaps before your intention arrives.

Why you start crying before you can explain what you’re feeling.

Why you react in ways that don’t match who you know yourself to be.

You’re not choosing those first reactions or behaviors. They’re choosing you. The deeper question is why they keep happening even when you want them to stop.

The brain doesn’t choose what’s healthiest or most aligned. It chooses what’s familiar. Familiar feels predictable. Predictable feels safe. Safe feels like survival.

If anger was the emotion that moved fastest in early life, anger becomes the quickest route out of discomfort. If avoidance filled the home, avoidance becomes the nervous system’s language of communication. If defensiveness once prevented vulnerability, it becomes protective armor.

These reactions represent well-worn neural pathways, patterned response grooves shaped over time. And unless those grooves are softened through safety, calm and repetition, the body will continue returning to them, even when the mind wants something different.

When this man learned how to calm his body before the hijack fully took over, change followed. Not overnight, but steadily. Over time, he was able to stay calm in the moment and remain in control because he wasn’t fighting his biology, and this meant the Wiser mind finally had room to lead again.

Reflection

What reaction shows up fastest for me under stress?

Do I make any facial expressions or body movements that represent my discomfort even when I know they aren't aligned with who I want to be in the moment? (Think along the lines of eye rolling, crossing arms, or waving fingers.)

____

____

____

____

____

____

Why You Don't Do the Things You *Want* to Do

One of the most confusing parts of being human is how deeply you can want something… and still find yourself unable to do it.

You want to exercise.

You want to spend time with friends.

You want to apply for the job, start the habit, learn the skill, take better care of yourself.

You know it would be good for you. You may even feel excited about it in theory. And yet, when the moment comes, your whole system says *no.*

This is where most people turn on themselves. They assume the problem is motivation, discipline, or follow-through. They tell themselves they *should* want it more, or *should* just push past the resistance. And when that doesn't work, they add frustration, self-judgment and pressure on top of an already overwhelmed HOS.

What they don't realize is this: when your body resists something you consciously want, it's rarely defiance. It's protection.

That resistance can come from different places.

Sometimes it's biological. The nervous system is already overloaded, running on stress, fatigue, or stored tension. From that state, *anything* extra, even something positive, feels like too much. The body says no because it doesn't have the capacity to say yes.

Sometimes it's belief-based. You may carry an old, quiet conclusion about what's allowed, worthwhile, or safe. A belief about effort, success, visibility or deservingness. The body responds to that belief automatically, and you may never notice it consciously without looking for it.

And sometimes it's a mindset loop. You notice resistance, interpret it as failure, get irritated with yourself, and try to force your way through. That irritation creates another stress response, which strengthens the resistance and reinforces the belief that something's wrong with you.

Different entry points. Same result. The body shuts the door.

Here's a simple example:

I worked with someone who desperately wanted to learn the piano. She wasn't interested in performing; she just wanted to learn some beautiful songs for enjoyment. She loved music. She loved the idea of sitting down and playing. And yet every time she tried, she avoided it. First, weeks passed by. Then months. She couldn't understand why something she *wanted* felt so hard to begin.

When we slowed it down, the answer became clear. Growing up, she had learned from her parents that doing things "just for fun" was a waste of time. Productivity equaled worth. Rest and play were indulgent, even irresponsible. That belief lived deep in her body.

So every time she sat down at the piano, her nervous system responded as if she were doing something wrong. Not consciously or logically, but she could feel hesitation. In addition, distraction was paired with her numerous attempts to become motivated and play.

Her body wasn't resisting music. It was protecting her from violating an old rule about who she was allowed to be.

Once that pattern was identified and challenged, the resistance began to dissolve. It wasn't about improving her discipline and forcing herself to play; it was about rewiring her belief system so she could remain true to the person she had become.

This is what's so important to understand: avoidance, procrastination, and freeze states are not laziness or fatigue. Most of the time, they're survival responses.

When the HOS senses too much pressure, uncertainty, or internal conflict, energy pulls inward. The body slows down, and movement and motivation become harder. Outwardly, it shows up as delay, distraction and self-doubt.

Overwhelm and distraction aren't character flaws. They're data. And when you understand that, the inner conversation changes. The question shifts from *What's wrong with me?* to *What is my system trying to protect me from?* That shift matters more than it seems, because the moment you stop fighting yourself, you create the conditions for change. Regulation comes first. Capacity follows. And behavior becomes possible again, not through force, but through alignment.

Reflection

Where in my life might hesitation be a signal of overwhelm or fear rather than lack of discipline?

____

____

____

____

____

____

Tool: Asking Your HOS Why

This journaling tool is for the moments when you want to do something that would be good for you, but your body resists in that gentle, somewhat hard-to-notice way. Just enough to stall, distract or shut things down.

Instead of pushing through that resistance, pause. Grab a pen and paper (best) or open your note-taking app on your phone.

First, name what you notice without judgment.

I want to do this... and something in me is saying no.

Then begin here.

1. Locate the resistance in the body

Before asking *why*, notice *where.*

Is it tightness in the chest? Heaviness in the limbs? Pressure in the head? A subtle pulling back? Fatigue?

Let your attention rest there for a few breaths. You aren't trying to change it. You're letting your HOS know it's been noticed.

2. Ask the body what it's protecting

Now, gently ask:

Why won't you...?

Write the first honest answer that arises. It may sound simple or even irrational. That's okay. This isn't a logical exercise; it's a listening one.

3. Ask again, with curiosity

Then ask:

Why?

Respond.

Then pause. You can repeat this many, many times. Asking why and just listening or reading the answer.

I often end up in a bit of discourse with my body, countering some of its beliefs. Become as creative or stay as narrow as you want with this. It's the connection that matters most.

4. Ask one final time

What would help my body feel better about taking this one step?

Not the whole thing or the perfect version.

Just the next tiny, doable step.

The answer might be reassurance.

It might be intentional rest for a specific amount of time.

It might be permission to go slowly.

It might be adjusting the expectation entirely.

Stop there. You aren't trying to override the nervous system. You're building a relationship with it.

Very often, once the body feels heard, the resistance lessens. Forward movement becomes possible because your nervous system no longer has to block you to stay safe. These are the first steps to developing trust within yourself.

This is how behavior changes in a sustainable way.

Reflection

Where in my life have I been trying to push behavior forward while my body was discreetly asking for safety instead?

What changes when I listen first?

____

____

____

____

____

____

The Marble Jar: The Space to Choose and Change

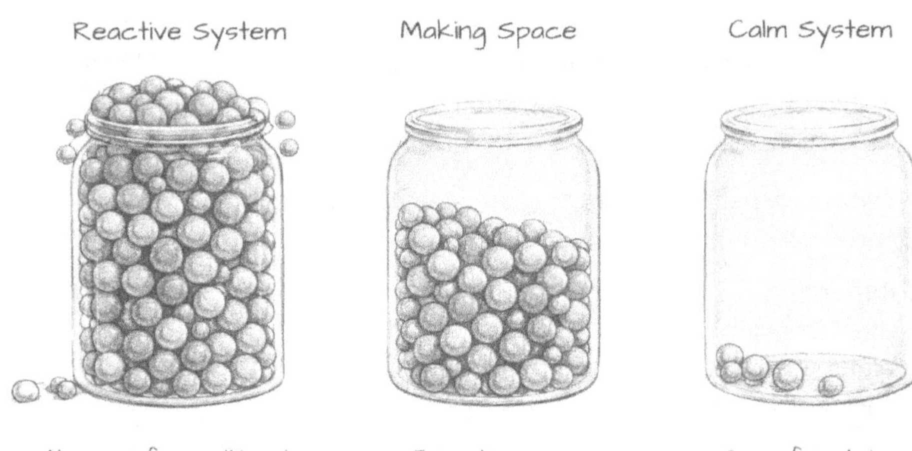

You can only change your behavior when your body has enough space to do something different. When your HOS is overloaded, even small choices feel hard, and new behaviors feel almost impossible to access. Calm helps in the moment, but capacity is what determines how much your HOS can actually hold, adapt to, and respond to across your day.

You can think about this the same way you would think about a glass of water. A glass can only hold so much before it overflows. The empty space in the glass is its capacity to hold what is being poured in. Your HOS works in much the same way. The more space you have inside your HOS, the more life you can take in without spilling over.

This is why behavior change isn't just about intention or discipline. It's about whether your body has room to respond before overflowing and defaulting into survival mode.

In relation to daily life, a simple way to imagine this is by pretending your mind and body are a jar of marbles.

When something happens to you — an emotion rises, a stress response turns on, or your body reacts to something in your environment — a marble goes into the jar as a signal to take action.

In a healthy, regulated system, the process completes itself. You feel what you feel, you take the action your body is asking for, and then the marble leaves the jar.

What you're left with is space.

That space is what allows you to respond to the world, adapt, and stay present with what's happening instead of being driven by it. It is often referred to as your adaptive reservoir because it is the reservoir of space within that allows your HOS to adapt to the circumstances efficiently.

The issue is that the way we live now doesn't support this process very well. We haven't evolved for this kind of modern lifestyle — we don't naturally regulate anymore. We override, suppress and push through.

So when emotions come up, whether in childhood or adulthood, and we don't actually take time to feel them, that marble of activation goes into the jar and stays there. When a stress response shows up, and the body wants to take action to protect us, and we don't follow through on that action, another marble goes into the jar.

You can describe this in many different ways. You can talk about it at a molecular level. You can talk about stress chemistry, the nervous system, or fascia. But the exact mechanism isn't what matters here.

What matters is that there's unresolved activation in the body, most likely decades of it. When there's energy that doesn't get to complete its cycle, it stays in the jar.

This often shows up as being wired but tired, consistently on edge, or feeling as though you don't have enough mental or emotional space to keep up with daily demands.

As more and more marbles build up, the body slowly loses its ability to take in more. There's less and less space left. Those marbles can make us feel heavy and burdened by the weight of our lives. They can also cloud our ability to see situations accurately. And if you listen to the language we use, we actually already know this. We say people have "lost their marbles."

What that really describes is a jar that has become so full that the next new marble spills out of the jar. It may even knock other marbles out with it. Now these marbles are rolling all over, causing internal chaos.

When that happens, people feel scattered and disoriented. They can't focus. They don't know what to do next. They become reactive and feel unstable because, in a way, they're now trying to run around collecting marbles and can't focus on anything else.

The goal isn't to get rid of the jar. And it's not to stop having marbles. The goal is to let marbles move in, acknowledge them as information, and then promptly allow them to move back out.

As we get older, we'll have a jar that contains more experiences. But every time an emotion comes up and we actually feel it, a marble comes back out. Every time a stress response shows up and we take the action the body is asking for, allowing the body to discharge what it has activated, a marble comes back out.

Sometimes that action is emotional.

Sometimes it's physical.

Sometimes it's setting a boundary.

Sometimes it's moving the body.

Sometimes it's slowing down long enough to let the nervous system settle.

Sometimes it's releasing what's already built up through movement, breath, or practices that help down-regulate the nervous system and clear stress chemistry, such as cortisol and adrenaline.

The more often you allow signals to come in and move through instead of staying stored, the more space you preserve inside your HOS.

That space is what gives you more energy and more flexibility. It gives you the capacity to respond instead of react.

There's another part of this that matters just as much: You don't have to wait until something goes wrong, or until your jar is full, to take marbles out.

This is why daily nervous system regulation matters so much. It's preventive. In the same way you brush your teeth every day so plaque doesn't slowly build up and turn into a cavity, you support your nervous system every day so stored stress doesn't slowly accumulate inside your body.

One of the simplest ways to make this consistent is to pair it with something you already do. I often suggest habit batching, which is linking a calming nervous system practice (a moment of taking a marble out) with an existing habit.

For example, when you brush your teeth at night, take a moment to help your HOS settle before sleep with a regulating practice. And in the morning, before the day begins to add new marbles to the jar, take another moment to create space.

That can look very simple. You might notice a sensation in your body and feel it gently. You might move into the day slowly, with mindful awareness. You might release tension with stretches. You might use breath, fascia work, nerve work or any practice that helps your HOS down-regulate and return to center.

The goal isn't to do more.

The goal is to create space. (That space will actually allow you to do *more* if you want to.)

When there's space in your jar, you have more room for choice. You have more room for intentional action. You have more room to engage with your life instead of just constantly managing what your body is carrying.

Reflection

Where in my life do I notice myself pushing through instead of listening to the needs of my body?

What would it look like to create one small daily moment to take a marble out before the day adds another one?

____

____

____

____

____

____

Choosing to Release Marbles

I'm offering you another option.

Regulation creates space, but real life is where marbles start to move. When an emotion comes up, it's an opportunity to remove a marble. The less you build a story around it, the more likely it is to move through and leave instead of being recycled back into the jar.

Tool: Feel It to Heal It

A 90-second emotional reset

Research on emotional processing suggests that when an emotion is allowed to move through the body without interruption, it can complete its natural cycle in about ninety seconds. Emotions are designed to rise, move through and settle. Think of it like light passing through glass: the glass doesn't resist the light, it simply allows it to pass.

When we allow emotional sensations to move through the body instead of interrupting them, they often resolve on their own. When they don't, it's most likely because the mind has stepped in — replaying the experience or adding interpretation — which keeps the emotion going.

This tool helps your nervous system complete the emotional loop without becoming trapped in a story.

How to Do It

If you can identify the emotion, name it gently.

"This is anger."

"This is sadness."

"This is fear."

You're not identifying with it. You are simply recognizing what's present. Bring your attention directly to how the emotion is showing up in your body.

Notice:

Where is it located?

Does it have a temperature?

A texture?

A color?

Is it still or moving?

Sharp or dull?

Expanding or shrinking?

Then repeat silently:

"I feel it."

Again and again, while you stay with the physical experience.

Remain with the sensation until it naturally softens.

For most people, this takes between thirty and ninety seconds when the emotion is being felt in the body rather than analyzed, explained, or woven into a story about who they are.

When the intensity settles, pause and ask yourself:

Does this emotion require any further action right now, or can I return to what I was doing?

This is how a marble leaves the jar. This is how calm creates emotional choice instead of emotional accumulation.

How Does Behavioral Awareness Help Us?

At this point, behavior stops being something you judge and starts becoming something you read.

Every reaction becomes information. Every hesitation becomes data. Every pattern becomes a message about what's happening inside your Human Operating System. Instead of asking, *Why did I do that again?* you begin asking, *What state was I in when that happened?* Behavior shifts from a verdict about your character to a doorway into awareness.

A sharp tone may point to pressure building in the body. Avoidance may point to overwhelm. Shutting down may point to protection. Overexplaining may point to uncertainty. When behavior is seen as communication rather than failure, shame softens and curiosity becomes possible. Awareness replaces self-criticism, and awareness is what allows change to begin.

But noticing is only half of the work.

The second use of behavior is intentional action. You can move your body to settle your body. You can slow your breath to soften reactions. You can step away before escalation or relax tension before speaking. Small regulating actions tell the nervous system it's safe enough to stay present. In this way, behavior becomes both the signal and the solution.

First, you read behavior to *understand* your state. Then you use behavior to *influence* your state.

This is the beginning of repatterning. You aren't trying to force yourself into becoming someone else. You're creating internal steadiness, so different actions naturally become available. Over time, these same principles support deeper change in identity and habits, but they only work reliably once this foundation is in place: awareness and regulation.

Behavior change doesn't begin with discipline. It begins with understanding what the system is doing and giving it a better place to operate from.

Now that you understand what behavior represents, you can begin to recognize it in everyday life. Once you know what to look for, these patterns appear everywhere — at work, in conversations, in relationships, and even in your own thoughts.

In the next chapter, we'll walk through real-life situations and illustrate how the Human Operating System unfolds in real time.

Chapter 8

How Your Patterns Show Up Everywhere: Relationships, Work, Parenting, Health & More

Your patterns are consistent because your nervous system is consistent. Once you can see the pattern across areas of life, you stop making it personal and start making it workable.

This chapter widens the lens from “me in a moment” to “me across my whole life.” You’re going to see how the same protection responses show up in communication, productivity, parenting, intimacy, health, money, habits, self-talk and boundaries — sometimes loudly, sometimes quietly, often in ways that have felt normal for so long they barely register. The point isn’t to diagnose yourself or overhaul your life. The point is to recognize your pattern as a system, because once you can name the system, you can interrupt it.

As you read, notice the places your body tightens. Where urgency rises. Where you over-function, shut down, people-please, avoid, control or go numb. Let those moments become information. This is pattern literacy. And it’s one of the fastest ways to regain leverage, because you’re no longer trying to “fix” one isolated behavior, you’re learning what your nervous system is protecting, and what it needs in order to choose differently.

For this reason, this chapter ends with a simple daily reset. When regulation becomes preventive rather than reactive, your patterns stop running the day before you even enter it. You begin your mornings with more capacity, which makes it easier to stay connected to your values in conversations, in work, in parenting and in your own body. This is where change becomes realistic: small, repeatable signals of safety that teach your system a new baseline.

After everything you've learned so far, you can likely now see more clearly how this current version of you came to be.

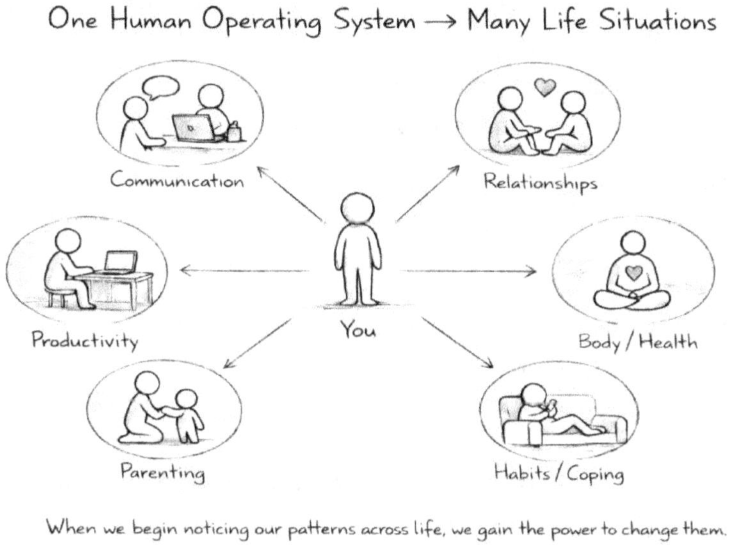

One Human Operating System → Many Life Situations

When we begin noticing our patterns across life, we gain the power to change them.

You can recognize how your nervous system learned how to respond before your thinking mind had a chance to choose. You can feel how calm restores access to your wiser, steadier mind. And you may already be noticing how much personal power returns when your body stops organizing your life around protection and begins organizing around presence.

I want to slow this moment down, because something important lives inside this understanding.

Genuine curiosity about your reactions, patterns and beliefs becomes one of the most sustainable ways to create real change. Curiosity opens the doorway to choice. When you notice what's happening inside your body and your mind with openness, rather than pressure or judgment, your system begins to experience safety with you. And safety creates the biological conditions that allow new responses to emerge.

This is also where compassion becomes a quiet turning point in growth and healing.

Offering yourself patience, understanding and real care regulates your nervous system in powerful ways. It teaches your body that it no longer has to work so hard to guard you from your own experience. For many people, learning how to meet themselves with kindness becomes one of the most meaningful and lasting shifts of their entire lives.

As you move into this next section, I invite you to hold one simple truth with you: Everything you are about to explore reflects how your system learned to survive.

With awareness, calm and choice now available to you, those same patterns become an invitation to grow, heal and evolve in ways that finally feel supportive from the inside.

Our Behavior Patterns Mimic Our Past, Yet They Do Not Define Who We Are

Now let's bring this out of theory and into real life.

By the time you reach adulthood, most patterns move quietly in the background of your life. They rarely announce themselves. They arrive through tone of voice, timing, habits, reactions and decisions. They appear in how you communicate, how you work, how you parent, how you connect and how you care for your body.

You rarely act this way on purpose.

Your nervous system, your beliefs, and your emotional history interpret each moment before your conscious mind has time to weigh in. Many people call this autopilot. I usually laugh and call it roboting. You likely understand exactly what I mean.

This chapter offers real-world windows into how long-standing stress and protection patterns often appear across everyday life. The purpose is simple. It helps you recognize behaviors that may have blended into your normal routine simply because you've never had this lens before.

You'll begin to notice where biology becomes behavior. Sometimes it appears quietly. Sometimes it shows up in more obvious ways. Every pattern makes sense once you understand how the HOS learned to protect you.

And once you begin to recognize these patterns, your awareness naturally becomes your leverage for change.

We begin with communication, because it's one of the fastest places nervous systems meet, and one of the clearest places old protective patterns tend to speak.

Stress Patterns in Communication

A client once described a meeting that, on paper, should have been completely ordinary.

He was leading a project team that was already stretched thin. A delivery had been delayed. A vendor issue had popped up overnight. A timeline that looked realistic two weeks earlier suddenly felt tight in a way that sat heavy on the shoulders before the meeting even started. He told me later that when he walked into the room, he could already feel that low hum and tension in his body that meant, *I'm behind and people are watching.*

The first few updates went fine. Then someone explained that one part of the timeline would probably slip by a few days because of something outside the team's control.

He felt it immediately. That tightening in the chest paired with pressure in his throat. The clenching of his jaw and the pursing of his lips he only noticed later, when we slowed the moment down together.

He cut in before the person finished explaining.

“So what’s the workaround?” he demanded.

They tried to answer. He interrupted again.

“Okay, but I need something more concrete than that.”

Another team member jumped in with an idea, a partial solution, something still rough around the edges. He corrected the numbers mid-sentence. His tone got sharper and his voice louder without him planning it. His body leaned forward over the table, not aggressively (or so he thought), just... intensely.

The room shifted immediately. (You know the way people pull back when they sense intimidation and danger.)

People started choosing their words more carefully. One person stopped offering ideas altogether and stuck to short status updates. Another glanced down at their laptop instead of looking up when they spoke. The conversation turned safe. Clean. Small.

At the end of the meeting, he walked out with a tidy list of issues and almost no solutions. What bothered him later was not what the team had said. It was how the room had felt.

He told me, “It was like everyone shutdown as the meeting went on. I didn’t realize it while I was in it, but looking back, I can see it. I was pushing. And the more I pushed, the less I got.”

When we unpacked the moment together, something simple became obvious. He had not been reacting to the delay. He had been reacting to what the delay meant inside his body.

For him, pressure had always been tied to identity. Being dependable. Being the one who could carry things when other people couldn’t. Being the person who stayed sharp so nothing slipped through. That belief lived deep inside him. It lived in his nervous system.

So when the timeline wobbled, his body interpreted it as threat to competence, threat to credibility, threat to safety in a role that mattered deeply to him. Thus, his HOS moved into control. He was not trying to dominate the room. His body was shifting into urgency and command because, at a biological level, this moment felt like survival. I am sure you can think of times in your life when projects or work deadlines felt like life or death.

As we continued to break down the experience, he said something that stuck with me.

"I thought I was leading. But I was actually protecting."

That one sentence became a guidepost. A new identity for how he wanted to lead under pressure.

Before walking into conversations that carried stress and pressure, he began taking a quiet moment at his desk. No big ritual. Just a few breaths and a check-in that became familiar to him very quickly. He also began using the micro-tool below during meetings when he noticed his body becoming activated and repeating silently to himself.

Calm is my power.

That pause gave his body just enough space to step out of urgency. And when his body settled, his voice changed. He still asked for accountability. He still held timelines and made decisions. What shifted was the quality of the space around him and within him.

People talked longer. Ideas stayed messy for a moment instead of being trimmed into something safe. Someone eventually said, "I have a half-baked thought here," and offered the solution that moved the project forward.

Nothing about his leadership skills changed that day.

His nervous system did. And once it did, the room could think again.

Micro Tool: The Signal Shift

Use this before a meeting or tough conversation, and anytime intensity rises during it.

Before You Begin

Lightly rub your thumb against the side of your index finger with slow, steady pressure. Notice the sensation on your finger and then your thumb.

Take one normal inhale and a slightly longer exhale. Let your jaw soften and your shoulders drop a fraction.

Keep attention on the sensation for a few seconds.

Then say internally:

Calm is my power.

You are setting the state your body will operate from before anything happens.

During the Conversation

If urgency, defensiveness, or pressure rises, repeat the same movement.

Finger to thumb. Longer exhale.

Calm is my power.

Pause half a beat.

Then respond to the actual words spoken, not the reaction your brain predicted.

You are not restarting the conversation. You are returning to your position.

What This Changes

The sensation pulls attention out of the threat story. The longer exhale reduces urgency. The phrase organizes behavior. Instead of reacting to pressure, you answer from stance.

People experience you as steady, clear and difficult to escalate because you are no longer participating in the reflex loop.

This tiny reset sends a signal of safety through the body, widening your perception. Wider perception creates space for choice. And choice is what changes communication patterns.

Small. Silent. Repeatable.

A tool that fits inside real moments.

Reflection

Can I remember a moment, at work or at home, when my reaction was stronger than the situation called for? What was said, and what did my body interpret it as in that moment? (Sometimes simply noticing that difference begins to loosen the pattern.)

If I could rewrite my next communication moment, the next piece of feedback, the next disagreement, or the next tense conversation, how would I want to show up?

What would it feel like to respond from calm instead of defensiveness?

Let yourself imagine it clearly. That picture becomes a guidepost your nervous system can begin to grow toward.

____

____

____

____

____

____

Stress Patterns in Work and Productivity (a.k.a. Procrastination): When Avoidance Is Your Nervous System Asking for Safety, Not Discipline

I sometimes laugh at myself when I avoid writing my own books. Because it is not a motivation problem. I care deeply. I want this work to land. I want it to help people understand their bodies differently. I want it to create real, lasting change.

I know exactly why this book matters to me.

And yet, there are moments when I can feel my body quietly — sometimes not so quietly — refusing to move toward the work.

It's subtle at first. I notice my mind drifting. I pick up my phone without thinking. I suddenly remember something small I should check. The dishes catch my eye. I wonder what my friend is doing. I stand up to use the bathroom. I glance at a stack of cards on the table and feel an odd pull to look through them. I even pause to check if the car is locked.

From the outside, it looks like distraction. From the inside, it feels different. It feels very much like my body doesn't want to step forward.

There's a very specific moment I've learned to recognize. It happens right before I open the computer and right before I turn to the page I know I need to work on. There's a quiet tension that grows in my chest. A small tightening in my stomach. A subtle resistance that doesn't sound dramatic at all, yet clearly says, *maybe later.*

My mind knows I want to write. My body is the one hesitating.

This is how a nervous system freeze often looks in real life.

Most people imagine freeze as complete shutdown. But in work and productivity, freeze usually shows up as gentle avoidance. It shows up as busyness. It shows up as perfectly reasonable micro-tasks that appear at exactly the moment you're about to move toward something that matters.

And what I've learned, both in my own life and in my work with clients, is that the body almost never freezes because the task is difficult. It freezes because the meaning attached to the task feels weighted... dare I say, "life-threatening."

Underneath my own hesitation live very familiar survival beliefs. What if this doesn't work? What if I can't write the way I want to? What if people don't understand what I'm trying to say? What if I put my heart into this and it doesn't land? What if I disappoint myself? What if I disappoint everyone else?

When you strip it all the way down, most work-related avoidance eventually circles the same two ancient threats.

Failure.

Rejection.

Both live very close to survival inside the nervous system.

Remember, before we had careers, performance reviews, publishing deadlines, or productivity apps, being rejected by the group and losing status or belonging meant real danger. The modern mind knows that a missed deadline isn't life-threatening. The nervous system doesn't run on modern logic, though. It runs on pattern, memory and emotional association.

When something matters deeply, when visibility increases, when responsibility feels real, and when other people are counting on you, the body often interprets that pressure as risk. And when the nervous system senses risk, it does what it has always done best. It tries to move you away from the discomfort. Distraction becomes protection, and avoidance becomes relief.

Scrolling, organizing, checking, tidying, researching one more thing, watching one more clip, answering one more message all serve the same biological purpose. They reduce the immediate emotional load that the body associates with stepping forward.

This is why telling yourself to be more disciplined rarely works for long.

The issue isn't willpower, it's safety.

Once I understood this in my own body, the way I work with procrastination changed completely. I stopped trying to force myself forward. I stopped trying to shame the hesitation away. I became curious about it instead.

And then I found something surprisingly effective. For me, one of the fastest ways to interrupt this pattern is to move my nervous system out of threat before I ask it to perform. Rather than pushing myself to start, I first let my body experience the feeling of finished.

I picture the page written. The paragraph complete. The small section closed. I let myself feel the quiet relief that comes when something meaningful is done. The excitement in my chest. The sense of space that opens when the pressure drops. The satisfaction of knowing I showed up to do what I said I would do.

When my body feels that state first, the tension releases almost immediately. It's as if my system hears, this is safe, this is manageable, this ends well. And once that signal lands, starting becomes much easier. And I don't have to force it because my body no longer feels like it has to protect me from the moment. We're now a team with shared enthusiasm for success.

This is the pattern most people miss. You don't move through avoidance by pushing harder. You move through it by changing the internal signal your nervous system is receiving. When the body feels safe, then mind and body can work as a team again, and forward motion becomes possible.

Micro Tool: Procrastination Buster

This is a simple, internal nervous system reset you can use anytime you feel yourself circling a task you care about by opening other tabs, reaching for your phone, or finding a dozen small reasons to delay what actually matters.

The key is to pause before you open the document, the screen, or the project.

Close your eyes for just a few seconds and imagine the task already finished.

Let your body notice the emotions or sensations of having completed the task.

The drop in shoulder tension.

The quiet relief.

The sigh of calm.

The easiness in your mind.

The subtle sense and smile of having followed through.

Stay with that felt experience for about ten to fifteen seconds.

This small moment works in a very specific way. When your body experiences completion first, your nervous system receives a new prediction about what is coming next. Instead of anticipating failure, pressure, or rejection, it begins to associate the task with safety, relief and resolution.

That shift brings your system out of protective avoidance and back into capacity.

Then, while that feeling is still present, ask yourself: **What is the very first small step I can take right now?**

As you begin that first step, continue to hold the feeling of completion. You really only need to get started, and most of the time, momentum will carry you from there.

This tiny reset sends a signal of safety throughout the HOS. Safety restores capacity. Capacity allows movement. Movement is what dissolves avoidance patterns.

It's gentle, practical and powerful — the kind of tool real humans can actually use in real life.

Reflection

When I notice myself drifting away from work that actually matters to me, what does my body feel like in that moment before the distraction begins?

Where do I sense the hesitation in my body — my chest, throat, stomach, shoulders, breath?

If I stay with that sensation for a few seconds instead of moving away from it, what story appears underneath it?

What am I afraid might happen if I truly give this work my full attention and energy?

If my body trusted that effort doesn't threaten my belonging, safety, or worth, how could I move into my tasks differently today?

____

____

____

____

____

____

Stress Patterns in Parenting: When Your Nervous System Is Raising the Child Alongside You

Parenting has a way of revealing the parts of ourselves we thought we'd outgrown. The small moments — the spilled cereal, the sibling argument, the whining right when you thought you had two seconds of quiet — look harmless from the outside. Yet when your system is running on poor sleep, accumulated stress, and the quiet belief that everything depends on you, those moments stop feeling small very quickly.

I worked with a parent who told me, while avoiding eye contact and almost whispering, "I don't recognize myself with my kids. I feel like I turn into a crazy person by the end of the day."

She cared deeply. She felt devoted to her family. She wanted to be patient. And yet her body kept taking over before her intention had a chance to arrive.

She described evenings that unraveled faster than she could catch. A raised voice she never planned to use. A tightness in her face that appeared before she even realized irritation was building. A constant sense of being surrounded by too many needs and too little internal space. Some nights it showed up as sharpness. Other nights it showed up as the opposite — a blank, distant feeling, as if everything were happening behind a sheet of glass.

"I feel overwhelmed before anything even happens," she said, "and honestly, before the day even starts."

I understood immediately.

When a parent lives inside a stress-primed nervous system, the body reacts long before intention has time to lead. Poor sleep intensifies this pattern. Sleep becomes available when the nervous system experiences safety, and many parents go to bed with a HOS that never fully powers down. Their body continues scanning, monitoring and carrying responsibility through vigilance.

As a result, the next morning, even after lying in bed for hours, their biology is already leaning toward protection before their feet touch the floor. When a day begins in survival physiology, even the sound of a small voice calling, "Mom?" from the other room can register like an alarm.

This experience reflects biology in action.

When the nervous system carries overload, the amygdala, the part of the brain that scans for threat, becomes highly sensitive to anything that feels unpredictable or out of control. Children, by nature, bring unpredictability. They move constantly. They change direction. They express emotion freely. They need presence, emotional availability and flexibility in real time.

A parent whose HOS holds the belief, *I have to hold everything together, or everything will fall apart* meets their child through a subtle lens of threat.

The body shifts into a low-level fight response. Not explosive aggression, but a simmering intensity that sharpens tone and shortens emotional range. The belief tightens the biology, and the biology narrows the available responses.

In that state, it becomes very difficult to access the part of you that understands, in a felt way, that your child is learning, exploring power, discovering choice, and practicing how to be human. Many parents never learned to recognize these behaviors as healthy expressions of development because their own nervous systems learned very different emotional rules. The challenge is rarely intellectual. It's physiological. You can't feel that truth when your body is bracing.

Calm restores that feeling.

Calm creates room in your internal marble jar.

When your jar has space again, more of you becomes available to your child. Perception widens. You begin to see your child as they are in this moment, rather than through exhaustion and pressure. Connection becomes accessible again. Reactivity loosens its grip. The old internal message — *it all depends on me* — loses its urgency, and support, pause and choice become available options.

Calm gives your nervous system the capacity to meet your child clearly.

And when your body returns to regulation, the parent you already are has space to show up.

You can't think your way into this state while your HOS is mobilized. Biology leads first. Cortisol and adrenaline need movement and release.

This is the brief reset I use with almost every overwhelmed parent I support, and it fits into real life, even if the only private space you have is a hallway or bathroom.

Micro Tool: The Reset Bounce

This is a short nervous-system release designed to move excess stress chemistry through the body and bring your regulation back online.

When you're able, step into another room. Stand tall and begin gently bouncing on your heels, allowing a small natural shake to move through your shoulders and arms. This rhythmic motion sends a powerful signal through the fascia and tells your body that the moment of urgency is passing.

As you bounce, add one long exhale through your mouth, as if fogging a mirror. Let the breath be slow and audible. That longer exhale activates the vagal pathways that guide your system toward regulation.

Then place one hand on your chest or over your heart. This physical contact anchors your nervous system in connection.

As your body settles, offer one simple internal cue:

"I'm allowed to slow down."

or **"I can respond from calm and alignment."**

Thirty seconds of this can change the direction of an entire interaction. You aren't fixing the day. You're giving your nervous system a way out of the fight response so you can access the parent you already want to be.

If you have kids watching you, this matters even more. The tools you practice become the tools they learn. A child who grows up around nervous-system repair grows up with an internal map for how to come back to themselves.

Reflection

When I think back to a recent moment with my child that felt more emotionally heated than I expected, what sensations were already present in my body before I spoke or acted?

If my nervous system had carried a little more space in that moment, what response would have felt most aligned with the parent I want to be for my child(ren)?

What would it feel like to offer myself the same understanding I so naturally extend to my child when they're still learning life lessons?

Can I forgive myself for the unaligned behavior and move towards finding more peace for future situations?

____

____

____

____

____

____

A Final Note for Parents: Your Calm Becomes Their Calm

There's something tender we rarely talk about in parenting, yet it shapes children more than our words, our rules, or our intentions ever could.

Children feel us.

They don't respond to what we say nearly as much as they respond to the state we're in while we're saying it. Remember that before they understand language, they understand nervous systems. Their bodies learn from our bodies. Their sense of safety grows from our sense of safety. Their emotional range stretches or contracts depending on the signals they receive from us.

This isn't a call to be perfect, emotionless, or endlessly patient. You're human. You'll get stressed, frustrated, overwhelmed and tired. That isn't the problem, and it never has been.

What I'm offering is something far more compassionate and far more powerful.

When you learn to calm your nervous system, you're not only reclaiming your own capacity, you're giving your children a different blueprint to grow up inside. You're showing them what it feels like to have a parent whose presence is reliable and intentional instead of stretched thin. You're offering them a regulated environment so their own biology doesn't have to brace in response to yours.

Children absorb what we embody. If we move through life in tension, they adapt around tension.

But if we learn how to settle, they learn what settling feels like. And when we breathe, they breathe.

Your calm becomes their foundation.

The work you're doing here isn't just for you. It's the gift your children will carry into their friendships, their classrooms, their adulthood, and eventually, their own families. Every time you pause, soften, exhale, or re-center yourself, you're not just breaking your own cycle; you're shaping the one they'll inherit.

Calm isn't a parenting technique. Calm is the legacy you pass down.

Stress Patterns in Intimacy and Love: When Two Nervous Systems Keep Missing Each Other

Most people walk into relationships believing communication is the problem, or compatibility is the problem, or the division of labor is the problem. But beneath all of those layers lives something quieter and far more powerful:

Two nervous systems trying to love each other while carrying years of unprocessed stress, belief filters and survival patterns.

This becomes most visible in intimacy — not the sexual kind, but the everyday kind.

The way partners meet each other at the end of a long day.

The way help is offered or withheld.

The way a small request lands heavier than it should.

The way tension builds in moments both people wish could feel simple.

I once heard someone say that when you enter a relationship, you're also entering a relationship with someone's nervous system. That lens explains far more than most people realize.

A client came to me carrying exhaustion she couldn't explain. Her home looked steady. Her relationship looked functional from the outside. There were no obvious crises shaping her days. And yet she lived inside a constant state of overwhelm that quietly made her feel like she was losing her mind.

There was no single moment that revealed what was happening. Instead, it was the accumulation of ordinary moments.

Each time she asked her partner for something small — help with dinner, a quick opinion, a few minutes of support — his response arrived edged with a passive comment or a sharp tone he seemed completely unaware of. When she tried to explain to him what she felt, irritation met her. Defensiveness followed quickly, displayed through huffy breaths or looking away.

Some days, the energy rose into anger. Other days, it collapsed into silence, with her husband's attention disappearing into a screen or into a withdrawal so thick it changed the feeling of the room.

Nothing was ever repaired. Nothing was ever resolved. And she learned that speaking up only made things harder.

So she stopped speaking up.

But silence didn't bring peace. The resentment still grew. The tension stayed in her body and refused to release. She could feel it in her belly, in her throat and in her diaphragm.

She was running the house, running the meals, running the logistics, running the parenting, and now quietly running the emotional management of the relationship as well. She became the relationship holder by default. And that invisible responsibility alone can slowly buckle a nervous system.

Her partner wasn't a villain or a narcissist. He was dysregulated, too.

He carried old belief filters formed before this relationship. Beliefs like *I'm a burden, I'm never quite enough, emotions make things worse, needing support means I'm failing*. For men in particular, these beliefs are often reinforced early and repeatedly: be steady, be useful, be competent, don't fall apart, don't need too much, don't show emotions other than anger.

Those beliefs weren't just his thoughts. They lived in his biology.

His nervous system stayed in a quiet version of survival, the kind that looks like low-grade irritability, emotional flatness, avoidance, distraction through screens and routines, or a slow emotional shutdown when things feel too charged.

He wasn't trying to hurt her. He simply didn't have the capacity to meet her. And when one partner doesn't have capacity, the other begins to carry the emotional load of two nervous systems.

No human body is designed for that.

At night, lying side by side in bed, their bodies didn't truly settle. They were two nervous systems subtly scanning one another for changes in breath, small shifts in posture, the hum of frustration that never quite gets spoken but is absolutely felt.

This is neuroception at work — the brain's subconscious threat-detection system.

Two activated nervous systems, feeding off each other all day and all night, looking for the proverbial bear.

Her sleep became light and fragmented. Her mornings felt heavy before the day even started. Fatigue became her baseline.

And none of this was about love. They loved each other deeply. This was about biology and belief.

When a nervous system stays organized around fight, flight, or freeze, closeness itself begins to feel risky. Requests start to feel like criticism. Needs feel like pressure. Conversations feel like traps and silence feels like abandonment.

The relationship slowly becomes shaped around protection instead of connection.

This is why couples feel like they're having the same fight over and over. Why small disagreements become exhausting because tone, timing, and facial expressions are constantly misread. And why it can feel like rejection when one partner moves toward connection while the other pulls away.

Often this lines up with familiar belief lenses: One nervous system learned early that staying connected requires expressing, explaining, reaching and repairing. The other learned early that staying safe requires minimizing, withdrawing, staying quiet and staying in control.

Both are survival strategies. Neither is wrong. They're simply incompatible unless their nervous systems themselves begin to change.

Calm is what changes this. Calm gives each partner the capacity to hear what is actually being said instead of what their body expects to hear. Calm allows disappointment to remain disappointment instead of danger. Calm allows requests to remain requests instead of accusations.

Calm gently loosens the childhood belief filters each person brings into the room, so the present moment can finally be interpreted as the present moment. Calm makes closeness feel safe again.

But calm has to begin in the body, not in the conversation.

You can't talk your way out of a survival state, especially not after chronic stress has set in.

Below you'll find a tool I teach to couples, particularly when one partner tends to pursue and the other tends to shut down — the exact pattern that continually played out for this client.

Micro Tool: The Side-By-Side Reset

This is a low-intensity co-regulation tool for moments when you and your partner feel tense, distant, irritated or emotionally overloaded.

It works particularly well when one person tends to shut down, and the other tends to reach.

Sit side by side on a couch, a bed, or two chairs turned in the same direction. Your bodies both face in the same direction. Your shoulders can be near, without needing to touch.

Each person places one hand on their own chest, the other hand in their lap.

Take one slow inhale through your nose, lifting your shoulders. Then take a longer, quieter exhale and allow your shoulders to drop. Do that twice.

As you breathe, let your attention rest on one steady physical sensation, the weight of your body on the seat, your feet on the floor, or the warmth of your own hand.

Please note that facing the same direction matters. Side-by-side positioning reduces social threat and tells the nervous system: *we are oriented together.* The longer exhale activates the vagal pathway and gently lowers defensiveness. Anchoring attention in sensation interrupts emotional momentum and gives the thinking brain space to come back online. In short, you are offering your HOS the highest opportunity to feel safe and listen.

After the second exhale, one person gently says:

"I'm feeling activated in my body." (Optionally, you might name the emotion directly or describe the actual sensations you feel — tightness, heat, pressure, restlessness, etc.)

Nothing else. No story. No explanation. No problem-solving.

The other person simply responds:

"I hear that."

Pauses for a breath. Then, still facing forward, asks:

"What would help you feel a little more supported right now?"

That's all. If tensions rise again in that moment, return to breath.

This tool lowers threat before it asks for connection. It allows presence without pressure. It creates safety for the body first, which is the only place real connection can begin.

For many couples, especially when stress is high, this side-by-side orientation works far better than face-to-face exercises. It respects how nervous systems actually regulate, particularly for partners whose biology associates emotional intensity with danger rather than relief.

Calm clears the space between two people long enough for compassion to return.

And compassion is what allows two nervous systems to finally meet again.

Reflection

In my relationships, where do I notice myself shutting down, people-pleasing, or pulling away, and what does my body feel in those moments?

If my system felt calmer and safer, what is one small, honest truth I wish I could share with someone I love?

Another Quick Note About Relationships: The Value of Repair and Response

One of the quiet foundations of relationship safety and long-term closeness comes down to two simple human capacities: repair and responding to bids for connection. Relationship researcher John Gottman describes repair as the way a couple finds their way back to each other after tension, misattunement, or emotional distance, and bids as the small, often subtle moments when one person reaches for connection through a comment, a look, a question, a touch or a shared observation.

From a nervous system perspective, both of these moments carry enormous weight. Repair tells the body that rupture does not equal abandonment. It restores safety after stress has passed and teaches your biology that closeness can survive discomfort. Responding to bids teaches the nervous system something just as powerful: ***I matter here.***

Each time a bid is received with presence, warmth, or simple attention, the body learns that connection remains available even in the middle of busy days, fatigue and emotional noise.

When calm becomes part of your daily rhythm, both repair and response grow easier. You hear the reach instead of the irritation. You feel the moment to come back together instead of staying guarded. Over time, these small acts of turning toward each other become the emotional infrastructure of a relationship. They create enjoyment, deepen trust, and build the kind of safety that allows two people to keep choosing each other again and again.

Stress Patterns for Health and Body Identity: When the Body Starts Speaking Because You Haven't Been Taught How to Listen

Most people assume stress lives in their mind. They believe anxiety is simply worry, overwhelm is simply busyness, and burnout is simply exhaustion. Yet the nervous system rarely speaks through thoughts first. It speaks through sensation — tightness, tension, fatigue, pressure, pain — and when a system has been carrying too much for too long, those sensations grow louder, more physical and impossible to ignore.

I spent years trying to understand why my body felt as though it were quietly unraveling, even while every test told me I was "fine." I sat in doctors' offices searching for answers. I experimented with supplements, diets and medications. I moved through scans and bloodwork, hoping someone could explain why I was living inside a body that felt as if it were turning against me.

But the truth was both simpler and more confronting to receive.

My body was functioning exactly as it was designed to. My body was reflecting what my nervous system had been storing for years, the unfinished stress cycles and emotional residue of my past. In other words, my marble jar was full, and often overflowing.

At first, the overflow was difficult to connect. My vision would blur unexpectedly during the day because stress chemistry surged through my HOS so quickly that it altered how my brain processed what I saw. My jaw and ears ached for months before I realized I was clenching through sleep, through traffic, even while standing in the shower. My teeth hurt, without even having to bite on anything, they actually just hurt — as though the pressure in my face needed somewhere to go.

Some nights, swallowing felt strained and awkward. The muscles in my throat tightened and refused to cooperate, leaving me frightened that something serious was unfolding. Heartburn became a frequent companion. Sleep turned unpredictable and shallow. My joints pulsed as though I had aged overnight. And when everything inside me tipped past capacity, a rash could appear within minutes — bright, hot irritation spreading across my skin, my body asking me to notice what I had been carrying.

The body always tells the truth before the mind feels ready to hear it.

And this truth reflects strength, intelligence and exquisitely protective biology.

When your nervous system detects threat, including emotional threat, it releases survival chemistry. Cortisol. Norepinephrine. Adrenaline. These exist as measurable substances circulating through the bloodstream, soaking into muscles, fascia and organs. They shift how the heart beats, how digestion moves and how the brain interprets the world.

When these chemicals rise occasionally, the body clears them with ease. When they remain elevated for long stretches of time, the body adapts by holding them. Whatever the body holds eventually expresses itself somewhere — through tight muscles, unsettled digestion, hormone disruption, skin changes, shallow breathing, racing thoughts, restless sleep, blurred vision, clenched jaws, pounding hearts and persistent headaches.

Few of us grow up learning that these frustrating, confusing, and lingering symptoms often represent the body waving a flag and saying, "You're carrying more than your system can process alone. I'm supporting you as best I can."

So many of us spiral into fear. We chase diagnosis after diagnosis. We lie awake on long nights, wondering what might be wrong inside us.

Until someone connects the dots and gently offers a different lens — your body is overwhelmed, not damaged — most of us keep treating surface symptoms while the deeper system beneath continues asking for support.

I want to be unmistakably clear here. Your body is never working against you. Your body is asking for your attention and, very often, regulation.

And regulation, far more than discipline, willpower, or grit, plays a foundational role in restoring physical health and supporting the larger healing picture.

When calm becomes a practice rather than an accident, the body finally exhales. Muscles soften. Stress chemistry clears. Digestion awakens. Sleep deepens. Tissue repairs. Hormones rebalance. Inflammation settles. Energy returns. Your biology begins to trust your leadership again, and it can return to what it does best — keeping you well.

Micro Tool: The Butterfly Settle

This is a simple, body-based way to help your nervous system release stored pressure when symptoms begin to rise in your body.

Use this often and especially when you notice your jaw tightens, your chest feels heavy, your stomach feels unsettled, your skin flares, your breath becomes shallow, or your body feels full in that familiar, overloaded way.

Cross your arms over your chest so your hands rest gently on your upper arms, like a loose and comfortable hug.

Begin tapping slowly from side to side. Left, right. Left, right. Keep the rhythm steady and soft, just enough for your body to feel the pattern.

As you tap, take one slow breath in through your nose and allow a longer breath out through your mouth. Let your shoulders drop as you exhale.

Then offer your body one simple sentence:

I am safe. My body is allowed to feel more at ease now.

Continue tapping for about twenty to thirty seconds.

This rhythm gives your nervous system bilateral input, the same organizing pattern your brain uses during walking, rocking and safe physical contact. It signals the survival system that the moment is passing and that your body no longer needs to stay braced.

Most people notice a small but meaningful shift. The breath drops lower. The jaw eases. The chest loosens. The urgency fades just enough for your HOS to come back toward balance.

This practice helps clear stress chemistry, settle the amygdala, and supports the physiology that allows healing, digestion, hormonal regulation and weight balance to function more effectively.

You aren't forcing your body to relax.

You're reminding it that safety is available again.

A Brief and Honest Note About Weight

There's a conversation most people never get invited into when it comes to weight. For many individuals, especially those who have lived under long-term emotional pressure, chronic responsibility, relational stress, or earlier life adversity, weight is beginning to be understood as more than a willpower issue.

A growing number of psychologists and nervous system-informed clinicians now view persistent weight struggle as deeply connected to how the body learns safety, protection and stress regulation. In other words, the body does not only respond to food. It responds to threat, pressure and emotional history.

From a nervous system perspective, protection can take many forms. Sometimes it looks like constant alertness. Sometimes it looks like numbing. And sometimes it looks like holding. When the body spends years living in high demand, emotional uncertainty, or unresolved stress, it adapts in the ways it knows how.

For some people, food becomes one of the fastest regulators available. For others, the body itself becomes part of the protection strategy, holding weight in ways that feel stabilizing to a system that doesn't yet experience life as fully safe.

This isn't a failure of discipline. It's an intelligent biological response shaped by lived experience and belief.

This does *not* mean weight is only emotional. And it doesn't mean every body is carrying the same story. It simply means that for many people, sustainable change becomes far more possible when calm, safety and self-trust are restored in the nervous system first. When the body begins to feel supported instead of pressured, the need for protection slowly softens. And from that place, both behavior and biology finally have room to change together.

Micro Tool: The Belief Unravel

This is a short writing practice designed to support physical symptoms and weight patterns by gently loosening the survival beliefs your nervous system has been organizing around for years.

Many symptoms are reinforced by the stories the body has learned to carry about responsibility, safety, rest, visibility, control and worth. These beliefs live far below conscious thought. They shape physiology long before logic has a chance to intervene.

This practice helps bring those beliefs into awareness without pressure or confrontation.

Open a journal or notes app and write one simple line.

My body feels stress and is reacting because it believes... (Let the sentence finish itself honestly.)

– that I have to hold everything together

– that slowing down creates risk

– that rest must be earned

– that I can't afford to fall behind

– that being seen leads to judgment

– that mistakes cost me belonging

Then write a second line.

Is this belief still true for who I am today?

Let the answer be quiet and uncomplicated. Even a gentle *"Sometimes,"* or *"Not anymore"* creates movement in the nervous system.

Then write one final line.

A belief that would support my body better right now is…

Choose something small and believable. Something your body can actually receive:

- I can pause for one minute.
- I don't need to carry this alone.
- My body is allowed to soften before the work is finished.
- Support is available to me.
- Rest doesn't remove my value.

Then stop.

This isn't about convincing yourself of a new identity, but rather interrupting the automatic survival story long enough for your nervous system to reclassify the present moment as safer than the past.

When belief begins to shift, physiology follows.

This is one of the quiet ways symptoms soften, habits change and the body slowly releases patterns that once felt necessary for protection.

Reflection

For body and health patterns:

When my body sends me signals such as tightness, pain, fatigue, or sudden flare-ups, what's usually happening in my life emotionally or relationally at the same time?

If my symptoms were allowed to be information instead of problems to eliminate, what might my body be asking me to change, protect, or finally tend to in my life?

For weight and protection patterns:

In moments when my body feels safest and most supported, how does my relationship with food, rest, and my body naturally shift without effort?

If my body no longer needed to use protection to keep me safe, what would feel different about how I care for myself and honor my worth?

____

____

____

____

____

____

A Few More Places Stress Patterns Hide in Plain Sight

By now, you may already be noticing something important.

The same nervous system patterns you see in communication, work, parenting, relationships and health don't stop there. They keep expressing themselves in other everyday places that often go unnoticed — not because they're small, but because they've been normalized.

Money is one of them.

For many people, financial behavior has very little to do with numbers and almost everything to do with safety. Avoiding bank accounts, delaying paperwork, overspending for comfort, over-controlling budgets, or feeling sudden urgency around money often reflects a nervous system responding to uncertainty, pressure, or old scarcity beliefs. The body reacts to financial responsibility the same way it reacts to relational or work stress — by trying to reduce perceived threat as quickly as possible.

Another quiet place where patterns live is in **physical pain and inflammation.**

When a nervous system remains activated for long periods of time, pain sensitivity increases, tissue recovery slows and inflammatory responses become easier to trigger. Many people experience flares in pain, migraines, digestive distress, autoimmune symptoms and chronic tension during emotionally demanding seasons because their physiology is responding to sustained stress chemistry.

Regulation doesn't replace medical care. It supports the internal conditions that allow healing systems (immune and lymphatic systems) to function more effectively for faster recovery.

Habits and coping behaviors are another clear window into nervous system states.

Scrolling, snacking, drinking, overworking, staying constantly busy, late-night streaming, over-training, or repeatedly reaching for distraction are not character flaws. They're fast, familiar ways the body has learned to settle, numb, or stabilize itself. When regulation becomes available inside the body, many habits soften naturally because the nervous system no longer needs external tools to do the work of calming.

Your relationship with yourself is another place patterns quietly shape daily life.

The tone of your inner voice — the pressure, the self-criticism, the constant evaluation of what you should be doing better — often reflects early belief filters about worth, safety and performance. A nervous system organized around survival tends to speak to itself in urgency. When calm increases, the inner environment softens. Self-talk becomes more accurate, more patient and far more supportive of sustainable change.

And finally, **boundaries**.

Difficulty saying no, over-explaining, over-giving, rescuing, or feeling responsible for other people's emotional states often come from a nervous system that learned early that safety lived in being helpful, agreeable, or invisible. Boundaries aren't only communication skills. They're biological permissions. A regulated system is better able to tolerate discomfort, disappointment and difference without collapsing into guilt or fear.

All of these patterns — money, pain, habits, self-talk and boundaries — follow the same principle you've seen throughout this chapter.

Behavior patterns are what reflect the state of the nervous system first.

When you begin to recognize your stress patterns showing up across many aspects of your life, one quiet truth becomes impossible to avoid: Your nervous system needs daily care.

Not occasional care. Not crisis care. Not something you reach for only after you feel overwhelmed, reactive, or exhausted. Regulation works in the same way brushing your teeth does. We don't wait for cavities to start brushing. We brush because we understand what happens when we don't.

And when there's already pain, inflammation, burnout, or chronic stress in the body, we don't do less. We become more consistent.

There's a well-known line often attributed to meditation teachers: "Meditate for twenty minutes a day — unless you're too busy. Then meditate for an hour." Beneath the humor is a very real biological truth. The more pressure your system is carrying, the more regulation it requires. This is not a lifestyle preference. It is maintenance for your nervous system.

Rather than offering another tool you only reach for when something feels wrong, I'm giving you a way to work with your body preventively. A daily practice that helps set your nervous system, your mind and your belief patterns before the world gets a chance to organize them for you.

Tool: 5-Minute Morning Stress Prevention Practice

A simple ritual to set your nervous system, mind and beliefs before the day begins.

The first few minutes of your morning hold more influence than almost anything you do later. After sleep, your nervous system is naturally closer to baseline, and your brain is more receptive to new signals. When you start from regulation, your day asks less of you because your system begins with more space.

Five minutes. One rhythm. One tone.

1) Wake Up the Body— 60 seconds

Before you do anything, stay right where you are. Feel the weight of your body in the bed. Let your body move the way it naturally wants to move, stretch, twist, yawn, roll your shoulders, reach your arms overhead like a cat waking up.

No "routine." No forcing. Just letting your body return to itself.

This is your first signal of safety: *I'm here. I'm in my body. I'm allowed to arrive slowly.*

2) Orient to the Room — 30 seconds

Now open your eyes and take in the real world. Slowly look around.

Let your eyes land on **three things you can see**, notice **two things you can feel** against your skin, and listen for **one sound.**

This brings your brain out of yesterday and into now — the place where regulation and decision-making actually work.

3) One Minute of Breath to Settle — 60 seconds

Place one hand on your chest and one on your belly (or wherever feels grounding).

Take a slow inhale through your nose... then a longer exhale through your mouth, almost like a soft sigh.

Do **three to five rounds** of this.

Nothing fancy. Just enough to tell your nervous system: *we're safe, we're steady, we're here.*

4) Stand + Open Your Body — 30 seconds

Stand up and do a simple sequence:

- **Reach up** toward the ceiling (full-body stretch) and take a big inhale
- **Slow squat** (even a half squat is perfect), bringing arms down like wings, and exhale
- **Reach up again** like you're making space in your ribs and chest

Repeat that **two to three times.**

This is the "turn on the lights" moment for your body — gentle strength, gentle openness, gentle aliveness.

5) Bathroom Reset: Teeth + Mirror Truth — 90 seconds

Now go to the bathroom, brush your teeth, and while you're there, look at yourself for a few seconds in the mirror.

Say something simple and direct — the kind of words your body can actually believe:

"Today will be a good day."

"I love myself."

“I value myself.”

“I honor myself.”

“I trust myself.”

Pick **one or two**, and mean them as you would a vow, not a performance.

6) Choose Your Intention for the Day — 30 seconds

Before you walk out, choose the tone of your day. One word is enough.

Ask: **What emotion do I want to live from today?**

Peace. Confidence. Patience. Courage. Steadiness. Playfulness. Presence.

Then set a simple intention line:

“Today, I lead with ___.”

And go.

Why This Works

This reset isn’t designed to perfect you. It prepares you.

It gives your nervous system a calm start, your mind a direction, and your beliefs a tone to follow — before the world starts pulling on you.

Now that you know how to begin your day from regulation on purpose, we move into the part most people try to rush, yet it is the very thing that makes transformation last. Insight opens the door. Regulation creates the space. Repetition is what makes change stick.

In the next chapter, you’ll learn how real change happens inside the Human Operating System, and why becoming who you want to be is less about effort and more about what you practice consistently. This is where growth becomes sustainable.

Chapter 9
The Science of Repetition

Change doesn't come from understanding yourself once. It comes from returning to calm often enough that your body learns a new normal.

Lasting change depends on repetition, not just motivation. In this chapter, you'll begin to understand how calm activates the brain's ability to rewire patterns, why modern life interrupts that process and how simple daily regulation practices retrain your nervous system over time. The goal isn't perfection, it's returning to calm often enough that new, aligned responses become automatic.

Why Calm Is the Foundation of Lasting Change

Before we go any further, there's one piece of science you need to understand, because it explains every single transformation you'll experience in this book: your brain and body change through repetition, not just inspiration.

Every thought, reaction, emotion and behavior you practice becomes a pattern your HOS stores. Neuroscientists call this **Hebbian learning, the idea that cells that fire together, wire together.** When you repeat something — a reaction, a belief, a behavior — the brain strengthens that pathway. It becomes faster, more automatic, more familiar. This is how your old patterns were built. Not through conscious choice, but through repeated survival responses your system practiced for years.

Building a New Path

You can think of your nervous system patterns like paths through a field.

The reactions you've practiced for years — worry, defensiveness, shutting down, overworking, people-pleasing — have been walked so many times that the trail is deeply worn. Your brain knows that path well, so it follows it automatically.

When you begin practicing calm responses instead, you aren't erasing the old path or pattern right away. You're simply beginning to build a new trail.

At first, that trail feels faint and unfamiliar. But each time you return to calm and choose a different response, you walk it again. Over time, the new path becomes easier to follow, until eventually it becomes the path your system takes naturally.

Building a New Path

Calm creates the space for choice,
and repetition turns that choice into a new pattern.

Here's the part most people aren't aware of, though: it's hard to rewire anything until the nervous system is calm enough to allow new wiring.

When your body is in survival mode — cortisol elevated, muscles tight, breath shallow, thoughts racing — the brain temporarily downshifts the regions responsible for learning and long-term change. This is biology doing its job. And as you understand by now, protection overrides growth every time.

This is where the marble Jar becomes useful again. The body needs space to learn something new. If the jar is already full, there's no room for flexibility. When you calm the nervous system, you create that space. The prefrontal cortex comes back online. Neuroplasticity increases, and the brain becomes flexible again. Emotional patterns loosen and release. Beliefs become more noticeable and movable. Behavior becomes available for change.

Calm doesn't just feel better. It makes you teachable.

And that's the formula. Not motivation. Not unrelenting self-discipline. Not trying harder.

Interestingly, it's often doing less to achieve more. An HOS that practices calm responses repeatedly becomes foundationally calm.

Every time you return to calm, even briefly, you reinforce the brain's pathway for clarity and deliberate choice. With repetition, this begins to shift your baseline. Stress no longer pulls you as quickly, and situations that once triggered automatic reactions feel more manageable. Gradually, you stop defaulting to old patterns and begin responding as the version of yourself you intend to be.

This is the science of becoming someone new.

The Human System Was Built for Regulation on Repeat

Regulation was supposed to be easier.

And the part I want you to remember when you start feeling like change is too hard, you're "too far gone," or you should be better at this by now.

Your body was not designed for zoo life.

Historically, regulation was built into the structure of being human. We moved constantly. We walked. We carried. We twisted. We sat on the ground. We climbed. We worked with our hands. We were outside. We tracked light, weather, seasons and sound. We didn't need to "make time" for nervous system health because nervous system health was the byproduct of how life worked.

And it wasn't only movement. Regulation lived inside the tribe. Singing, drumming, dancing, laughter, shared meals, shared work, shared grief. Community wasn't a bonus. It was part of the nervous system's blueprint.

Even wisdom had a place. Elders. Mentors. Wise people. Those who held perspective when someone else was lost in fear or pain. Humans were surrounded by cues of connection, land, meaning and belonging — the very cues that tell the nervous system: you are safe enough to soften.

This is why your body still responds so quickly to nature, rhythm, movement and presence. It's not *woo*. It's memory. Your biology recognizes what it was built for.

The modern problem isn't that you're broken or fragile. The modern problem is that regulation is no longer embedded into life. At present, if you want the benefits that used to come naturally, you have to practice them intentionally. You have to reintroduce what your nervous system expects.

This is why repetition matters so much. You aren't forcing a new personality. You're restoring a forgotten operating system.

When you practice body awareness and regulation repeatedly, the script begins to rewrite itself. Your body stops bracing as the default. Your reactions stop being the first response. Your body starts trusting you again.

Success!

The Only Thing You're Really Building Is a Daily Relationship With Your Own Signals

If you take nothing else from this chapter, take this: the goal is not to stay calm all day. The goal is to return to calm on repeat.

This is nervous system hygiene, the way brushing your teeth is hygiene. As we've touched on in a previous chapter, you don't wait for cavities to begin brushing. You brush because you understand cause and effect. And if you already have cavities, you don't give up. You double down.

Regulation works the same way. The more life you're carrying, the more consistent the practice becomes. Not because you're failing. Because you're human.

You're building a daily relationship with your body's signals. You're becoming someone who can feel activation without obeying it. Someone who can notice the stress response without turning it into identity. Someone who can hear what the nervous system is asking for and respond with leadership instead of pressure.

And that kind of self-leadership becomes automatic the same way everything else became automatic: repetition.

The Strategic Reasons to Stay Regulated

If I haven't convinced you yet, let me share this in the most simplistic way I know how.

This is the truth of the Human Operating System:

You practice **calm for the health of your body** because your organs, hormones, immune function, digestion, sleep, inflammation and energy all depend on whether your nervous system believes it's safe enough to repair.

You practice **calm for emotional stability** because emotions are meant to move, not stack. Calm gives your feelings somewhere to land without flooding your entire day. And it gives you the space to let those emotions move through you instead of consume you.

You practice **calm for your mind** because your brain can't focus, innovate, problem-solve, or prioritize well when it's busy scanning for threat. Calm is what returns your brilliance and your authenticity.

You practice **calm for your relationships** because people can't feel you when you're in protection mode. Calm helps you hear accurately, respond to bids, repair faster and stay connected without protecting yourself from everything.

You practice **calm for your beliefs** because beliefs don't change in a defended body. Calm is what makes your inner world flexible enough to update the old stories you built in survival.

And you practice **calm for your everyday life** because life isn't only meant to be managed. It's meant to be felt. Enjoyment, presence, laughter, patience, creativity, desire and gratitude all require a nervous system that's not fighting invisible danger all day.

This is why we practice. This is why repetition matters. This is why the smallest tools count. Because the version of you that feels steady, clear, capable and deeply alive isn't created through one breakthrough.

It is created through what you practice.

Tool: EFT – Emotional Freedom Technique

The best way to calm and rewire simultaneously — a repetition-friendly practice that regulates the nervous system and softens old patterns.

EFT (Emotional Freedom Technique) is a simple practice that combines gentle tapping on certain points of the body with awareness of what you are feeling. Variations of tapping on the body have been used in different healing traditions for a long time.

When you tap on these points while paying attention to a feeling or belief, your body receives calming signals through the nervous system.

The tapping helps the body settle while your mind stays aware of what is happening inside you. As the body relaxes, the intensity of the emotion often begins to soften.

When the body feels safer, the brain becomes more flexible. This is the state where learning and pattern change can occur.

This is why EFT fits so well with the science of repetition. You aren't trying to convince yourself of anything. You are helping the body calm down while the mind notices the pattern.

Over time, repeated practice teaches the nervous system something new. Activation no longer has to lead to shutting down, avoiding, or protecting. Instead, the system learns that it can stay present.

Each time you calm your system this way, it's like taking a marble out of the jar and creating a little more space inside your HOS. Now you have more room for choice.

How to Use EFT as a Calm-First Repetition Practice

Choose one pattern you notice repeating — a reaction, belief, or body response.

Name it simply and honestly. For example:

"This tight pressure in my chest."

"This urge to shut down."

"This feeling that everything depends on me."

"This fear that I will get it wrong."

Begin tapping gently with two fingertips on each point below.

Tap each point **5–10 times** while keeping your attention on the body sensation or belief you named.

Move through the points in this order:

Inner Eyebrow: At the inner edge of the eyebrow, near the bridge of the nose.

Side of the Eye: On the bone just outside the outer corner of the eye.

Under the Eye: On the bone directly beneath the eye.

Under the Nose: In the small space between the bottom of the nose and the upper lip.

Chin: In the crease between the lower lip and the chin.

Collarbone: Just below the collarbone, slightly to either side of the center of the chest.

Center of the Chest: The middle of the upper chest over the sternum.

Top of the Head: The crown of the head.

As you tap, repeat a simple calming statement such as:

"This is a stress pattern in my system."

"My nervous system is trying to protect me."

"I am safe enough right now to let this soften."

Continue tapping through the points for about **20–40 seconds.**

Then pause.

Take one slow breath and notice what has shifted in your body. Even a small change — a softer breath, less tension, a little more space — means your nervous system is beginning to regulate.

This is how new responses begin.

EFT is not about forcing emotions away. It is about helping the body settle while your mind stays aware of what is happening.

With repetition, the nervous system learns a different response to activation. Instead of tightening or shutting down, it begins to return to calm more quickly.

Over time, that calm response becomes the new pattern.

There are many variations of EFT that include additional tapping points or longer sequences. I've found these locations to be the most helpful for calming and rewiring, but if the practice resonates with you, I encourage you to explore it further.

Why EFT Supports Real Rewiring

Repetition is what trains your system.

Each time you meet activation with calm awareness instead of bracing, avoiding, or suppressing, your nervous system learns something new. Over time, the brain updates what it expects to happen in those moments.

This is how a calm response becomes more natural — not through force, but through repeated experiences of safety.

Reflection

What changed in my body, even just a little?

What do I notice now that I didn't notice before?

____

____

____

____

____

____

And So It Begins...

You now find yourself at a turning point — the place where everything you've learned stops living in your mind and starts living in your body. It's where calm stops being an idea and becomes a daily experience. It's where regulation becomes less of a practice and more of a reflex.

It's where you shift from knowing who you want to be to *living* as that person in the moments that matter.

People often imagine transformation as a dramatic moment — a revelation, a breakthrough, some cinematic turning of the page. But in real life, transformation is subtle. It's measured in microscopic choices, repeated again and again, until they grow strong enough to become automatic. You don't suddenly become the person who responds calmly instead of exploding. You practice it. You rehearse it. You train your system into it the same way you would strengthen a muscle.

And eventually, the practice becomes the identity.

This is the part most self-help books never tell you. You can't change by forcing yourself to be different. You change by teaching your body what "different" feels like, and different — when it's authentic — **feels good.**

Every time you regulate, even for a few seconds, you're showing your biology a new pattern. A pattern that your system will eventually choose on its own.

Your nervous system is always learning. The only question is: what is it practicing today?

The rest of this book is about turning regulation into something you return to without thinking — the way you reach for your seatbelt or stop at a red light. Automatic. Baseline. Familiar.

Chapter 10
The Eye of the Storm

The storm never actually stops. You simply learn to stand steady at its center — and enjoy it.

What if the goal was never to control life... but to finally feel steady enough to enjoy it?

We live in an ever-changing world — brilliant, chaotic, fast, distracting, breathtaking. And somewhere inside all of it, each of us faces a choice: to keep surviving our lives or to start actually living them.

We can hide in the familiar excuses, pressure, and busyness that keep us numb and distracted, or we can admit that something in us is craving more.

More joy. More truth. More ease. More connection. **More life.**

Eventually, we reach a moment when we realize the old way isn't working. A moment when something inside whispers, *I want different*. Not a new schedule or hobby, but a different experience of being alive — one that feels intentional instead of automatic, aligned (almost magical) instead of reactive.

The truth is, most of us were never taught how to access that kind of shift. No one explained how much our nervous system and survival beliefs shape our choices, relationships, confidence and capacity. Instead, we learned to work harder, stay alive and keep going.

Over time, that whisper gets louder. Sometimes it takes illness, divorce, job loss, or deep exhaustion to finally hear it clearly. You realize you're tired of worry, stress and tension being your baseline. Tired of waiting for the next mistake, the next conflict, or the next shoe to drop.

You begin to notice that what you labeled "normal" is actually exhaustion. What you called "stress" is actually survival. And what you assumed was your personality — the irritability, overthinking, shutdowns, anxiety — was never you at all. It was your biology asking for a different way of living.

This is the turning point.

The Path to Change

The shift you're craving doesn't come from throwing your life away and starting over. It comes from learning to read your body's language differently. Awareness opens the door to change — but your nervous system has to be calm enough to let you walk through it.

This is also where the Wiser, Aligned part of you begins to wake up.

When your nervous system settles, the information coming from your body becomes clearer. Sensations and emotions that once felt urgent or overwhelming become informative. This is the difference between being driven by your body from protection and listening to it from safety.

Calm isn't something you're born with. It's something you practice. A pattern your nervous system learns through repetition, through body awareness, and through small, real moments of regulation woven into everyday life.

When calm becomes familiar, you begin to glimpse your true self — not the zoo self that learned to survive inside invisible enclosures, but the self that chooses from preference instead of protection.

As a result, you finally feel awake. Awake to your life. Awake to your truth. Awake to the parts of you that have been waiting for you to remember who you *truly* are.

That's the difference between reacting to your life and choosing to live it.

When Calm Becomes the Place You Live From

Calm gives you the power to start living life on your terms. Not a life without chaos — no one gets to have that — but a life where chaos doesn't get to run you.

The storms will always exist. They show up as deadlines, tough conversations, challenging relationships, unknowns, curveballs, politics, pressure and heartbreak. They swirl the way the weather swirls.

But calm lets you stand in the center of it.

From that place, you gain the clarity to see what's actually happening instead of being tossed around by every emotional gust. You can respond without fear, listen without judgment and hold your boundaries without shaking. The world can keep moving — fast, loud, unpredictable — and you don't lose yourself in the spin.

Calm gives you the power to remain yourself under pressure, when life pulls at every edge you have.

Over time, it becomes the new set point that everything else is built on. Not because life suddenly becomes easier, but because you're finally meeting it from inside your own steadiness. You know your worth, and you trust that you can find your way forward, no matter the circumstances.

People love to talk about "creating the life they want," but you can't create anything from a body stuck in protection. You can chase. You can hustle. You can prove your worth day after day. You can achieve more than anyone thinks possible.

But you can't create an authentic life from fear.

Creation requires openness and curiosity. And openness requires safety. This is why calm is the entry point to an aligned life.

And here's a truth that often goes unspoken: you deserve a life that feels like it belongs to you.

From Protection to Presence

When you calm your system, something shifts — almost as if the world becomes ten degrees brighter. A sense of possibility slips back into the body. And as you keep returning to calm, you begin to see how much of your life was shaped by protection rather than preference. You will realize that nothing was ever wrong with you; your body was just doing exactly what it was designed to do to keep you safe.

What I know now is this: calm isn't about isolation and quiet. Calm is about connection — to your body, your intuition, your truth, and the incredible intelligence running through you. It's the doorway into authenticity.

Authenticity, in my experience, is one of the most powerful and deeply satisfying states a human can live from.

It's the place where your body, your beliefs, your attention and your choices begin pointing in the same direction. Some people call it finding your true north.

Your nervous system is always organizing your reality around what feels safe, believable, and permitted — not what you wish for, but what your body actually trusts you can manage. And when your body is calm, your Wiser mind comes back online. It's the part of you that can notice, question, reframe and choose.

From there, old stories begin to loosen. Long-held assumptions soften. Your beliefs gain just enough flexibility to update. And slowly, your choices begin to come from who you're becoming instead of who you once had to be.

Life starts to change because you come back into alignment with yourself.

From that place, life doesn't just become manageable — it becomes alive. Enjoyable. *Expansive.*

A Lived Truth

For those of you reading this who feel that adventure is frightening and change is nearly impossible, it's not because you're incapable. You feel this way because your body learned, somewhere along the way, that change meant danger.

I know that survival belief well. I called it Generalized Anxiety Disorder. I called it stress. I called it "the nothing."

There was a season in my life when I was so depressed that I truly didn't care whether I lived or died. I wanted to disappear because I was exhausted from living inside a nervous system — and beliefs — built on fear, responsibility and the constant pressure to prove my worth.

On the outside, I looked capable. High-functioning. The strong, confident mother of two beautiful kids. People praised me for keeping it together.

Inside, I was falling apart.

And although I didn't realize it at the time, none of that was my personality or my truth. It was biology and survival beliefs running the show. It was my nervous system — and my inner knowing — asking for a different way of living. I just didn't yet understand its language.

This is why I tell people not to justify their suffering by pointing to the parts of life that look fine on the outside. Your body *always* knows where you're living out of alignment. And it's *always* trying to guide you back toward yourself.

I believe deeply that happiness isn't the reward at the end of life. Happiness is the point of life. And the path that keeps you connected to it is built through calm, curiosity and the courage to be honest about who you really are.

When I finally committed to regulating my Human Operating System — not perfectly, but consistently — everything began to shift. Not overnight. But steadily. I could feel the difference between a life organized around fear and a life guided by alignment.

And I want that for you.

You don't need fixing. Yet I imagine there is far more possibility inside you than your survival patterns have ever allowed you to see.

It's time to allow calm to become your access point, curiosity to become your path to aligned choices, and courage to become the threshold you cross into your own freedom.

If you take anything with you from this book, let it be this:

Your body isn't standing in the way of your future. It's the doorway to it.

Once you feel what it's like to live from calm — to think, choose, and relate from a nervous system that finally feels safe enough to open — you'll no longer be willing to build your life from anything other than your truth and your joy.

Chapter 11
A Thank-You to Your Body

Self-understanding and gratitude for your body bring you to the threshold of transformation; from here, life opens into limitless possibility.

Before you move on, pause for a moment and bring your attention back to your body. Notice your breath moving in and out. Notice the steady rhythm of your heart. Notice that you are here — alive inside your body, right now.

Take a moment to feel gratitude for your body. For the way it has carried you through every season of your life. For the way it learned to protect you when you didn't yet have the tools. For the way it worked to keep you alive while offering guidance the entire time.

Your body has been doing its absolute best for you every single day of this journey.

At the heart of this work is a simple truth: your body isn't something to overcome. It's the partner you're learning to listen to. And when you begin meeting your body and your Human Operating System with gratitude and intention, you truly become whole.

Trust begins to grow.

First, **your body begins to trust you**. As you stop overriding its signals and start responding with attention instead of pressure, it no longer needs to shout to be heard. Sensations settle more quickly because they've been acknowledged.

Then **you begin to trust your body**. Feelings that once seemed like problems begin to feel like information. Tightness becomes guidance. Activation becomes energy. Instead of fearing what you feel, you learn how to work with it.

And finally, **you begin to trust yourself**. Because you understand what's happening inside you, life no longer requires constant control. You can move forward without needing certainty. You know you can meet whatever arises and respond with intention, authenticity and steadiness.

This is the partnership calm creates — a relationship between awareness and sensation where your inner world no longer competes for your attention. Trust, gratitude and calm begin to reinforce one another. Appreciation softens the nervous system. Safety restores clarity. Calm becomes something you return to through connection rather than effort.

And now you understand why that matters.

Calm is power.

Thank you for choosing to do this work for yourself. By understanding your inner world more honestly, you are choosing a calmer, more connected, and more authentic way of living. And just as stress moves through families, workplaces, and communities, so do safety, kindness and joy.

Imagine what becomes possible when more people recognize their own value and their capacity to feel well and live well.

I'm genuinely excited for what comes next in your life. Stay connected with people who are learning and growing alongside you. We aren't meant to do this work alone.

This life is meant to be lived, explored and enjoyed.

Blessings to you — and to your body, the miracle that made this entire journey possible.

About the Author

Nicole Hope Sylvester studies and teaches the connection between stress, the nervous system and human behavior. A former school teacher, fitness instructor, and mother of two, she became deeply curious about how the body and mind interact after experiencing anxiety and depression in her own life.

While teaching children, Nicole began noticing how early experiences shape the way people respond to stress later in life. This insight, combined with her own search for answers, led her to explore how the nervous system, body awareness, and the pressures of modern society influence the way we think, feel and behave.

Drawing on years of teaching movement, anatomy, and body awareness, Nicole helps people understand the biological signals constantly moving through the body and the powerful role the nervous system plays in everyday life. She developed the concept of Stress Fluency, a practical framework that helps people recognize how stress influences emotions, decisions and behavior.

Nicole believes stress has become a silent epidemic in modern society. By translating the science of stress and physiology into clear, practical tools, her work helps people feel steadier, think more clearly and respond to life with greater confidence.

She sees this work as part of a larger cultural shift toward better understanding the human body and the role it plays in how we experience life.

Nicole lives in California with her family and continues to teach and write about stress, the nervous system and the intelligence of the human body.

If the journey within these pages resonated with you and you'd like to continue exploring these ideas at a deeper level, you're invited to join a growing community of people committed to living with greater calm, clarity and intention.

Scan the QR code below to stay connected and explore more resources.

APPENDICES

Continue the Conversation: Resources for Deeper Understanding

If something in this book resonated with you, these authors expand the same ideas through different lenses — biology, emotion, behavior, relationships and resilience. Follow the topic that feels most helpful right now. You don't need all of them at once.

Understanding the Body & Stress

Bessel van der Kolk — *The Body Keeps the Score*
How experiences live in the body and why safety changes healing.

Peter Levine — *Waking the Tiger*
How the nervous system stores survival responses and releases them through regulation.

Gabor Maté — *When the Body Says No*
The connection between emotional patterns, stress and physical health.

Aimie Apigian — *Biology of Trauma*
A clear, body-first explanation of how trauma is stored in the nervous system and shapes patterns, reactions, and health.

Nervous System & Regulation

Stephen Porges — *The Pocket Guide to the Polyvagal Theory*
Why your body constantly scans for safety and how that shapes behavior.

Deb Dana — *Anchored*
Practical ways to work with your nervous system in daily life.

Linda Graham — *Resilience*
How the brain learns steadiness through repeated experience.

Emotions, Beliefs & Change

Marc Brackett — *Permission to Feel*
Understanding emotions so they guide instead of overwhelm.

Bruce Lipton — *The Biology of Belief*
How perception and belief influence biology and behavior.

Relationships & Social Behavior

John Gottman — *The Seven Principles for Making Marriage Work*
Research-based understanding of connection and repair.

Vanessa Van Edwards — *Cues*
Reading people and communicating with clarity and confidence.

Understanding Human Behavior Patterns

Malcolm Gladwell — *The Tipping Point*
How small behaviors create large changes in individuals and groups.

You don't have to read everything. Pick the ones that make you feel curious or hopeful because that's usually where growth begins.

Common Emotions and What They May Be Signaling

This chart offers a simple way to understand what different emotions may be signaling beneath the surface. These signals are not perfect or universal, but they can help you move from reaction into curiosity as you listen to your inner world with more awareness and compassion.

Anger: A boundary may feel crossed, or something feels unfair.

Anxiety: The nervous system senses uncertainty or possible threat.

Sadness: Something meaningful may feel lost or unfulfilled.

Shame: A belief about worth or belonging may be activated.

Fear: The body is preparing for danger or change.

Frustration: Something important feels blocked or out of control.

Guilt: A behavior may not match personal values.

Jealousy: A desire or unmet need may be present.

Overwhelm: The nervous system (HOS) may be carrying too much activation.

Joy: The body senses alignment, connection or meaning.

Curiosity: The system feels safe enough to explore something new and look at a thought or situation with a different perspective.

Calm: The nervous system feels safe and regulated.

Emotions are not problems to eliminate.

They are information from your Human Operating System.

The Toolbox

The practices in this book were designed to be simple enough for real life and powerful enough to create change over time. This section gathers them in one place so you can return to them easily whenever you need support, clarity or a way back to yourself.

Body-Based Tools

Tool 1: Orienting with Your Eyes

A 10–20 second reset for an activated mind.

When animals return to safety, the first thing they do is look around.

This is a biological cue that says, "The danger passed."

Your nervous system responds the same way.

How to Do It:

Sit or stand comfortably.

Gently move your eyes to the far right and pause for 2–3 seconds.

Move your eyes to the far left and pause again.

Then let your eyes scan the room slowly, landing on a few objects. (You can even choose your favorite color to help narrow down your search.)

Let your breath follow naturally. Repeat until you feel calm kick in, even just a little.

Why It Works:

Side-to-side eye movement engages the vagus nerve and lowers sympathetic charge.

Scanning the room tells your system you are not in danger right now.

This is one of the fastest ways to interrupt activation.

(You can even practice this with your eyes closed, as you try to fall asleep. Of course, you can't "see" anything in the dark with your eyes closed, so just pretend to see the room.)

Tool 2: Hand-To-Heart + Slow Breaths

A direct signal of safety through the heart and diaphragm.

Your body responds to warmth, pressure and slow exhalation. These cues activate the part of the vagus nerve responsible for calming and reconnecting you to the present moment.

How to Do It:

Place and gently press one hand on your chest.

Place the other hand on your lower ribs or belly.

Inhale gently through your nose.

Exhale longer than your inhale, even by one second.

Let your hands remind your body that you are safe enough to calm a little. Repeat as long as necessary.

Why It Works:

Touch communicates safety faster than language. A longer exhale activates the calming branch of the vagus nerve. Together, they create a physiological shift toward regulation.

This is a powerful tool when negative emotion rises quickly.

Tool 3: Centering Through Your Feet

A grounding practice that brings your system back into the present moment.

Your feet have dense nerve endings that communicate directly with your balance and stability systems. Gentle movement here restores a sense of orientation, "I am here. I am supported."

How to Do It:

Stand and feel the weight of your feet on the ground.

Slowly roll from heel to toe.

Then roll side to side, noticing pressure change.

Let your breath settle as your body finds balance.

Why It Works:

Grounding through the feet interrupts spiraling thoughts, pulls attention out of the future and reorients your nervous system to the present moment.

It's subtle but deeply stabilizing — especially when thoughts are racing.

Micro Tool: The Reset Bounce

(quick activation release through movement)

This is a short nervous-system release designed to move excess stress chemistry through the body and bring your regulation back online.

When you're able, step into another room. Stand tall and begin gently bouncing on your heels, allowing a small natural shake to move through your shoulders and arms. This rhythmic motion sends a powerful signal through the fascia and tells your body that the moment of urgency is passing.

As you bounce, add one long exhale through your mouth, as if fogging a mirror. Let the breath be slow and audible. That longer exhale activates the vagal pathways that guide your system toward regulation.

Then place one hand on your chest or over your heart. This physical contact anchors your nervous system in connection.

As your body settles, offer one simple internal cue:

“I’m allowed to slow down.”

or “I can respond from calm and alignment.”

Thirty seconds of this can change the direction of an entire interaction. You aren’t fixing the day. You’re giving your nervous system a way out of the fight response so you can access the parent you already want to be.

If you have kids watching you, this matters even more. The tools you practice become the tools they learn. A child who grows up around nervous-system repair grows up with an internal map for how to come back to themselves.

Micro Tool: The Butterfly Settle

(calming the body so it can heal)

This is a simple, body-based way to help your nervous system release stored pressure when symptoms begin to rise in your body.

Use this often and especially when you notice your jaw tightens, your chest feels heavy, your stomach feels unsettled, your skin flares, your breath becomes shallow, or your body feels full in that familiar, overloaded way.

Cross your arms over your chest so your hands rest gently on your upper arms, like a loose and comfortable hug.

Begin tapping slowly from side to side. Left, right. Left, right. Keep the rhythm steady and soft, just enough for your body to feel the pattern.

As you tap, take one slow breath in through your nose and allow a longer breath out through your mouth. Let your shoulders drop as you exhale.

Then quietly offer your body one simple sentence.

I am safe. My body is allowed to feel more at ease now.

Continue tapping for about twenty to thirty seconds.

This rhythm gives your nervous system bilateral input, the same organizing pattern your brain uses during walking, rocking and safe physical contact. It signals the survival system that the moment is passing and that your body no longer needs to stay braced.

Most people notice a small but meaningful shift. The breath drops lower. The jaw eases. The chest loosens. The urgency fades just enough for your HOS to come back toward balance.

This practice helps clear stress chemistry, settle the amygdala, and supports the physiology that allows healing, digestion, hormonal regulation and weight balance to function more effectively.

You aren't forcing your body to relax.

You're reminding it that safety is available again.

EFT – Emotional Freedom Technique

The best way to calm and rewire simultaneously — a repetition-friendly practice that regulates the nervous system and softens old patterns.

EFT combines gentle tapping on specific points of the body with focused attention on what's happening internally. It works by pairing cognitive awareness with physical regulation signals sent through the nervous system.

From a physiological perspective, EFT stimulates somatosensory pathways while the brain is holding an emotional or cognitive target in awareness. This pairing works to reduce threat activation and emotional charge, allowing the nervous system to return to regulation more quickly.

When the body feels safer, the brain becomes more flexible.

That is the state where learning and pattern change can occur.

This is why EFT fits directly into the science of repetition. You aren't trying to convince yourself of anything. You're helping the body settle while the mind updates.

Over time, repeated use teaches the nervous system that activation doesn't require collapse, avoidance or protection. It requires presence.

That is how new responses become possible.

How to Use EFT as a Calm-First Repetition Practice

Choose one pattern you notice repeating — a reaction, belief, or body response.

Name it simply and honestly. For example:

"This tight pressure in my chest."

"This urge to shut down."

"This feeling that everything depends on me."

"This fear that I will get it wrong."

Begin tapping gently with two fingertips on each point below.

Tap each point 5–10 times while keeping your attention on the body sensation or belief you named.

Move through the points in this order:

Inner Eyebrow: At the inner edge of the eyebrow, near the bridge of the nose.

Side of the Eye: On the bone just outside the outer corner of the eye.

Under the Eye: On the bone directly beneath the eye.

Under the Nose: In the small space between the bottom of the nose and the upper lip.

Chin: In the crease between the lower lip and the chin.

Collarbone: Just below the collarbone, slightly to either side of the center of the chest.

Center of the Chest: The middle of the upper chest over the sternum.

Top of the Head: The crown of the head.

As you tap, repeat a simple calming statement such as:

“This is a stress pattern in my system.”

“My nervous system is trying to protect me.”

“I am safe enough right now to let this soften.”

Continue tapping through the points for about 20–40 seconds.

Then pause.

Take one slow breath and notice what has shifted in your body. Even a small change — a softer breath, less tension, a little more space — means your nervous system is beginning to regulate.

This is how new responses begin.

EFT is not about forcing emotions away. It is about helping the body settle while your mind stays aware of what is happening.

Repetition trains your system. Each time you meet activation with calm awareness instead of bracing, your nervous system learns something new.

There are many variations of EFT that include additional tapping points or longer sequences. I’ve found these locations to be the most helpful for calming and rewiring, but if the practice resonates with you, I encourage you to explore it further.

Awareness and Reflection Tools

Tool: The Belief-Catching Practice

When you notice a strong reaction to your circumstances, ask yourself:

What belief might be running right now?

Is this a survival belief or an aligned belief?

How does believing this help me right now?

Survival beliefs formed to protect you.

Aligned beliefs support the life you're consciously building.

You don't need to change anything in that moment. You only need to notice which belief is guiding you. Because once a belief becomes visible, it stops acting like truth and becomes something you can work with.

Tool: A Somatic Check-In to Gain Clarity and Release Old Emotions

You don't need a journal or a long ritual. You need a moment of noticing and curiosity.

The goal of this practice is simple: to let the emotion move through, and to notice whether a belief is present without trying to solve it.

This isn't belief work. This is emotional completion and information gathering.

Here's the rhythm:

First, notice the initial signal.
This is the earliest moment something shifts. A tightening in the face, shoulders or stomach. A change in breath. A wave of emotion. A quick uncomfortable thought. This is the moment before the reaction gains momentum, when awareness still has room.

Next, feel what's happening in your body.
Not the story. Not the explanation. Just the sensation itself. Stay with it as sensation rather than meaning. Many emotions are unfinished experiences looking for completion, and the body releases them far more efficiently when they are met with presence rather than analysis.

Then, notice what it seems connected to, if anything.
Sometimes a belief becomes obvious, like calm is unsafe or I always mess things up. Sometimes there's no clear belief at all, only activation. Both are completely valid. You aren't required to name or fix anything here. You're simply noticing what shows up.

Ask gently, "Is this now, or is this then?"
This question creates space. It helps you sense whether your body is responding to the present moment or to an old emotional memory surfacing to be released. Many reactions aren't warnings. They're echoes.

Allow the emotion to complete.
Instead of suppressing or distracting, let the sensation rise, peak and soften. This teaches your HOS that it's safe to feel without needing to act or control. When emotions are allowed to finish, they lose their energy.

Finally, choose your next step from calm.
Once the body settles even a little, clarity returns. You can sense whether action is actually needed, a boundary, a conversation, a pause, or whether nothing needs to be done at all because the emotion has already passed.

If a belief surfaces and continues to repeat, that's information you can work with later.

If nothing lingered, the emotion simply needed completion.

The purpose of this is to listen long enough to know what, if anything, requires attention and start gathering data about what's happening in your HOS.

Tool: Rehearsing Safety (Visualization Practice)

Think of a moment that usually creates a reaction in you.

A conversation. A presentation. A pause in a relationship. Something real.

Close your eyes and picture the moment as if it's happening right now.

Let it feel real enough that your body responds.

Notice what shows up.

Tightness. Breath-holding. Emotion rising.

Now stay with both:

the imagined moment...

and the feelings you are experiencing in your body.

Keep the scene in your mind while you gently regulate your body.

Soften your shoulders. Take a slow breath out.

Let your body feel the emotion and settle at the same time.

You're not trying to remove the feeling.

You're showing your system that the feeling can move through you ... and you're still safe.

Stay there for a few breaths.

Then come back to the present moment.

Repeat this a few times.

Each time, your body learns something new: *I can feel this... and remain steady and present.*

I can be in this situation... and still be assured of myself.

With this tool, visualization introduces the experience. Feeling the emotion allows the pattern to complete. Calm begins to rewrite the belief.

Tool: Asking Your HOS Why

This journaling tool is for the moments when you want to do something that would be good for you, but your body resists in that gentle, somewhat hard-to-notice way. Just enough to stall, distract or shut things down.

Instead of pushing through that resistance, pause. Grab a pen and paper (best) or open your note-taking app on your phone.

First, name what you notice without judgment.

I want to do this... and something in me is saying no.

Then begin here.

1. Locate the resistance in the body

Before asking why, notice where.

Is it tightness in the chest? Heaviness in the limbs? Pressure in the head? A subtle pulling back? Fatigue?

Let your attention rest there for a few breaths. You aren't trying to change it. You're letting your HOS know it's been noticed.

2. Ask the body what it's protecting

Now, gently ask:

Why won't you...?

Write the first honest answer that arises. It may sound simple or even irrational. That's okay. This isn't a logical exercise; it's a listening one.

3. Ask again, with curiosity

Then ask:

Why?

Respond.

Then pause. You can repeat this many, many times. Asking why and just listening or reading the answer.

I often end up in a bit of discourse with my body, countering some of its beliefs. Become as creative or stay as narrow as you want with this. It's the connection that matters most.

4. Ask one final time

What would help my body feel better about taking this one step?

Not the whole thing or the perfect version.

Just the next tiny, doable step.

The answer might be reassurance.

It might be intentional rest for a specific amount of time.

It might be permission to go slowly.

It might be adjusting the expectation entirely.

Stop there. You aren't trying to override the nervous system. You're building a relationship with it.

Very often, once the body feels heard, the resistance lessens. Forward movement becomes possible because your nervous system no longer has to block you to stay safe. These are the first steps to developing trust within yourself.

This is how behavior changes in a sustainable way.

Micro Tool: The Body Belief Unravel

(before old beliefs carry you away)

This is a short writing practice designed to support physical symptoms and weight patterns by gently loosening the survival beliefs your nervous system has been organizing around for years.

Many symptoms are reinforced by the stories the body has learned to carry about responsibility, safety, rest, visibility, control and worth. These beliefs live far below conscious thought. They shape physiology long before logic has a chance to intervene.

This practice helps bring those beliefs into awareness without pressure or confrontation.

Open a journal or notes app and write one simple line.

My body feels stress and is reacting because it believes... (Let the sentence finish itself honestly.)

– that I have to hold everything together

– that slowing down creates risk

– that rest must be earned

– that I can't afford to fall behind

– that being seen leads to judgment

– that mistakes cost me belonging

Then write a second line.

Is this belief still true for who I am today?

Let the answer be quiet and uncomplicated. Even a gentle *"Sometimes,"* or *"Not anymore"* creates movement in the nervous system.

Then write one final line.

A belief that would support my body better right now is...

Choose something small and believable. Something your body can actually receive:

I can pause for one minute

I don't need to carry this alone

My body is allowed to soften before the work is finished

Support is available to me

Rest doesn't remove my value

Then stop.

This isn't about convincing yourself of a new identity, but rather interrupting the automatic survival story long enough for your nervous system to reclassify the present moment as safer than the past.

When belief begins to shift, physiology follows.

Reset Tools for the Moment

Tool: FLOW Set Point (the most powerful tool in this book)

The FLOW Set Point is a simple, body-first sequence you can use in real time to regain clarity, choice and direction. It isn't about forcing calm or fixing your thoughts, but rather helping your nervous system settle enough for your Wiser mind to come back online.

Use FLOW anytime you feel rushed, reactive, overwhelmed, foggy, or off-center. Its purpose is practical and immediate: restore enough regulation so you can choose your next step intentionally instead of reacting from habit or stress.

FLOW doesn't eliminate emotion. It gives you access to yourself while emotion is present.

F — Focus and Feel

Begin by paying attention to the body.

Instead of asking, *What's wrong?* or *What should I do?,* bring your awareness to your body.

Where do you feel activation right now?

Tightness? Pressure? Heaviness? Heat? Restlessness? Emotions?

You aren't analyzing. You're locating.

This step shifts you out of mental spin and into the present moment, where change actually happens.

L — Listen and Learn from sensation and emotion

Next, listen without fixing.

Let the sensations and emotions be exactly as they are.

Discomfort, irritation, sadness, fatigue or tension aren't problems to solve — they're signals.

You don't need to explain them or attach a story. Simply acknowledge what's present.

Listening tells the nervous system it has been heard, which often softens the internal alarm on its own.

O — Orient and Open through regulation

Next, help your system reorient to now.

Use a simple regulating cue:

- a longer exhale
- gentle movement
- grounding through your feet
- hands to heart or ribs
- orienting your eyes to the room

In more emotional moments, this may mean staying with the feeling long enough for it to release, without searching for meaning or belief.

The goal is not perfect calm.

The goal is enough regulation to remind the body: *there is no immediate threat right now.*

This is the bridge between body and mind. Choosing to orient and calm the body in the moment will also allow you to open the door (or window) to more internal information, as well as see the external world with more clarity.

W — Witness and Wonder

From this steadier place, witness the moment and what's really happening.

Thoughts may still be present, but now you're observing them rather than believing them automatically. You notice what your mind is saying without arguing, correcting, or following it. Just get curious about them.

Perspective returns here. You can see the aspects of the situation more accurately now.

You're no longer inside the reaction.

You're observing it.

(Some people find it helpful to imagine a bird's-eye view — as if you're gently watching the moment instead of being pulled into it.)

Set Point — Set your next aligned action

Only now do you choose what comes next.

Not the whole day.

Not the whole solution.

Just the next aligned step.

This might be:

- a boundary
- a conversation
- a task
- rest
- movement
- or choosing a belief or intention that fits the present moment

The Set Point keeps choice grounded and manageable, so the nervous system doesn't become overwhelmed again.

FLOW is about building self-awareness.

It's about knowing how to return to center — again and again — and taking agency in the moment.

Each return compounds. Small moments of regulation lead to clearer decisions, steadier behavior and a life that feels more intentional over time.

Tool: Feel It to Heal It

A 90-second emotional reset

Research on emotional processing suggests that when an emotion is allowed to move through the body without interruption, it can complete its natural cycle in about ninety seconds. Emotions are designed to rise, move through and settle. Think of it like light passing through glass: the glass doesn't resist the light, it simply allows it to pass.

When we allow emotional sensations to move through the body instead of interrupting them, they often resolve on their own. When they don't, it's most likely because the mind has stepped in — replaying the experience or adding interpretation — which keeps the emotion going.

This tool helps your nervous system complete the emotional loop without becoming trapped in a story.

How to Do It:

If you can identify the emotion, name it gently.

"This is anger."

"This is sadness."

"This is fear."

You're not identifying with it. You are simply recognizing what's present. Bring your attention directly to how the emotion is showing up in your body.

Notice:

- Where is it located?
- Does it have a temperature?
- A texture?

- A color?
- Is it still or moving?
- Sharp or dull?
- Expanding or shrinking?

Then repeat silently:

"I feel it. I feel it. I feel it."

Again and again, while you stay with the physical experience.

Remain with the sensation until it naturally softens.

For most people, this takes between thirty and ninety seconds when the emotion is being felt in the body rather than analyzed, explained, or woven into a story about who they are.

When the intensity settles, pause and ask yourself:

Does this emotion require any further action right now, or can I return to what I was doing?

This is how a marble leaves the jar. This is how calm creates emotional choice instead of emotional accumulation.

Micro Tool: Procrastination Buster

This is a simple, internal nervous system reset you can use anytime you feel yourself circling a task you care about by opening other tabs, reaching for your phone, or finding a dozen small reasons to delay what actually matters.

The key is to pause before you start the work.

Close your eyes for just a few seconds and imagine the task *already finished.*

Let your body notice the emotions or sensations of having completed the task.

The drop in shoulder tension.

The quiet relief.

The sigh of calm.

The easiness in your mind.

The subtle sense and smile of having followed through.

Stay with that felt experience for about ten to fifteen seconds.

This small moment works in a very specific way. When your body experiences completion first, your nervous system receives a new prediction about what is coming next. Instead of anticipating failure, pressure, or rejection, it begins to associate the task with safety, relief and resolution.

That shift brings your system out of protective avoidance and back into capacity.

Then, while that feeling is still present, ask yourself: *What is the very first small step I can take right now?*

As you begin that first step, continue to hold the feeling of completion. You really only need to get started, and most of the time, momentum will carry you from there.

This tiny reset sends a signal of safety throughout the HOS. Safety restores capacity. Capacity allows movement. Movement is what dissolves avoidance patterns.

It's gentle, practical and powerful — the kind of tool real humans can actually use in real life.

Micro Tool: Side-by-Side Reset

(regaining connection in relationships)

This is a low-intensity co-regulation tool for moments when you and your partner feel tense, distant, irritated or emotionally overloaded.

It works particularly well when one person tends to shut down, and the other tends to reach.

Sit side by side on a couch, a bed, or two chairs turned in the same direction. Your bodies both face in the same direction. Your shoulders can be near, without needing to touch.

Each person places one hand on their own chest, the other hand in their lap.

Take one slow inhale through your nose, lifting your shoulders. Then take a longer, quieter exhale and allow your shoulders to drop. Do that twice.

As you breathe, let your attention rest on one steady physical sensation, the weight of your body on the seat, your feet on the floor, or the warmth of your own hand.

Please note that facing the same direction matters. Side-by-side positioning reduces social threat and tells the nervous system: *we are oriented together.* The longer exhale activates the vagal pathway and gently lowers defensiveness. Anchoring attention in sensation interrupts emotional momentum and gives the thinking brain space to come back online. In short, you are offering your HOS the highest opportunity to feel safe and listen.

After the second exhale, one person gently says:

"I'm feeling activated in my body." (Optionally, you might name the emotion directly or describe the actual sensations you feel — tightness, heat, pressure, restlessness, etc.)

Nothing else. No story. No explanation. No problem-solving.

The other person simply responds:

"I hear that."

Pauses for a breath. Then, still facing forward, asks:

"What would help you feel a little more supported right now?"

That's all.

This tool lowers threat before it asks for connection. It allows presence without pressure. It creates safety for the body first, which is the only place real connection can begin.

For many couples, especially when stress is high, this side-by-side orientation works far better than face-to-face exercises. It respects how nervous systems actually regulate, particularly for partners whose biology associates emotional intensity with danger rather than relief.

Calm clears the space between two people long enough for compassion to return.

And compassion is what allows two nervous systems to finally meet again.

Micro Tool: Signal Shift

Use this before a meeting or tough conversation, and anytime intensity rises during it.

Before You Begin

Lightly rub your thumb against the side of your index finger with slow, steady pressure. Notice the sensation on your finger and then your thumb.

Take one normal inhale and a slightly longer exhale. Let your jaw soften, and your shoulders drop a fraction.

Keep attention on the sensation for a few seconds.

Then say internally:

"Calm is my power."

You are setting the state you will operate from before anything happens.

During the Conversation

If urgency, defensiveness, or pressure rises, repeat the same movement.

Finger to thumb. Longer exhale.

Calm is my power.

Pause half a beat.

Then respond to the actual words spoken, not the reaction your brain predicted.

You are not restarting the conversation. You are returning to your position.

What This Changes

The sensation pulls attention out of the threat story. The longer exhale reduces urgency. The phrase organizes behavior. Instead of reacting to pressure, you answer from stance.

People experience you as steady, clear and difficult to escalate because you are no longer participating in the reflex loop.

This tiny reset sends a signal of safety through the body, widening your perception. Wider perception creates space for choice. And choice is what changes communication patterns.

Daily Practice Tools

5-Minute Morning Stress Prevention Practice

A simple ritual to set your nervous system, mind, and beliefs before the day begins.

The first few minutes of your morning hold more influence than almost anything you do later. After sleep, your nervous system is naturally closer to baseline, and your brain is more receptive to new signals. When you start from regulation, your day asks less of you because your system begins with more space.

Five minutes. One rhythm. One tone.

1) Wake Up the Body— 60 seconds

Before you do anything, stay right where you are. Feel the weight of your body in the bed. Let your body move the way it naturally wants to move, stretch, twist, yawn, roll your shoulders, reach your arms overhead like a cat waking up.

No "routine." No forcing. Just letting your body return to itself.

This is your first signal of safety: *I'm here. I'm in my body. I'm allowed to arrive slowly.*

2) Orient to the Room — 30 seconds

Now open your eyes and take in the real world. Slowly look around.

Let your eyes land on **three things you can see**, notice **two things you can feel** against your skin, and listen for **one sound.**

This brings your brain out of yesterday and into now — the place where regulation and decision-making actually work.

3) One Minute of Breath to Settle — 60 seconds

Place one hand on your chest and one on your belly (or wherever feels grounding).

Take a slow inhale through your nose... then a longer exhale through your mouth, almost like a soft sigh.

Do **three to five rounds** of this.

Nothing fancy. Just enough to tell your nervous system: *we're safe, we're steady, we're here.*

4) Stand + Open Your Body — 30 seconds

Stand up and do a simple sequence:

- **Reach up** toward the ceiling (full-body stretch) and take a big inhale
- **Slow squat** (even a half squat is perfect), bringing arms down like wings, and exhale
- **Reach up again** like you're making space in your ribs and chest

Repeat that **two to three times.**

This is the "turn on the lights" moment for your body — gentle strength, gentle openness, gentle aliveness.

5) Bathroom Reset: Teeth + Mirror Truth — 90 seconds

Now go to the bathroom, brush your teeth, and while you're there, look at yourself for a few seconds in the mirror.

Say something simple and direct — the kind of words your body can actually believe:

"Today will be a good day."

"I love myself."

"I value myself."

"I honor myself."

"I trust myself."

Pick **one or two**, and mean them as you would a vow, not a performance.

6) Choose Your Intention for the Day — 30 seconds

Before you walk out, choose the tone of your day. One word is enough.

Ask: **What emotion do I want to live from today?**

Peace. Confidence. Patience. Courage. Steadiness. Playfulness. Presence.

Then set a simple intention line:

"Today, I lead with ___."

And go.

Why This Works

This reset isn't designed to perfect you. It prepares you for the day.

It gives your nervous system a calm start, your mind a direction and your beliefs a tone to follow — before the world starts pulling on you.

Closing Practice: Gratitude for the Body

Gratitude becomes more powerful when it is felt in the body rather than only thought about in the mind. This practice helps you reconnect with the quiet intelligence that supports you every day.

Begin by sitting comfortably and taking one slow breath. Let your shoulders soften and allow your attention to settle in the center of your chest.

Place a hand over your heart and think of something that naturally brings a small sense of appreciation. It could be a person, a peaceful moment, a beautiful place in nature, or simply the fact that you are alive today. Stay with that feeling for a few breaths and allow the sensation of gratitude to grow warm in your chest.

Now imagine that feeling gently spreading through your body.

Offer a quiet moment of gratitude to your heart for beating steadily and carrying life through you.

Offer gratitude to your lungs for breathing in fresh air and releasing what your body no longer needs.

Offer gratitude to your brain and nervous system for helping you learn, adapt and move through the world. Offer gratitude to your stomach and digestive system for turning food into energy and nourishment.

Offer gratitude to your arms and hands for everything they help you create, hold and care for.

Offer gratitude to your legs and feet for supporting you and carrying you through your life.

You don't need to rush this. Let each moment of appreciation land gently in the part of the body you are acknowledging.

Finally, return your attention to your heart. Notice how your body feels after offering appreciation to the systems that support you every day.

Take one slow breath and allow the feeling of gratitude to settle through your whole body before continuing with your day.

5–4–3–2–1 Nature Sensing Practice

The nervous system regulates best when attention returns to the present moment. *Nature provides one of the easiest ways to do this.* When the mind is busy or the body feels overwhelmed, gently bringing your senses back online can calm the system and restore balance.

This simple exercise helps your body shift out of overload by reconnecting you with your surroundings.

Step outside if possible and slowly move through the following:

5 – Notice five things you can see.

Look for colors, shapes, or movement in the natural world around you. Leaves, clouds, light through branches, the texture of bark.

4 – Notice four things you can feel.

The ground under your feet, the air on your skin, the warmth of the sun, or the texture of a leaf or stone.

3 – Notice three things you can hear.

Birds, wind through trees, distant sounds, or the quiet rhythm of your own breath.

2 – Notice two things you can smell.

Fresh air, soil, plants, water, or the subtle scent of the environment around you.

1 – Notice one slow breath.

Let the inhale expand gently and allow the exhale to release tension from the body.

This simple sensory reset reminds your Human Operating System that you are safe in the present moment. Even a minute of conscious sensing can calm the nervous system and bring the body back toward balance.

Key Concepts

Human Operating System (HOS)
Every person runs an internal system that shapes how they think, feel and respond to life. This system includes the nervous system, emotional responses, beliefs and patterns that develop through experience.

Calm Is a Biological State
Calm is not simply a mindset. It is a physiological state where the nervous system feels safe enough to relax, allowing the brain to think clearly and learn.

Awareness Comes Before Change
Patterns cannot change until they are seen. Learning to notice body signals, emotions and beliefs creates the opportunity for different choices.

Beliefs Shape Behavior
Beliefs act like internal rules the brain uses to predict what is safe, possible and expected in the world.

Repetition Rewires the System
The brain and nervous system change through repeated experiences. Practicing calm responses over time creates new patterns.

Calm → Curiosity → Courage → Authenticity
When the nervous system settles, curiosity becomes possible. Curiosity builds understanding, which creates the courage to live more authentically.

The Eye of the Storm
Life will always contain uncertainty and pressure. The goal is not to eliminate the storm but to learn how to experience life from a calm center where choices become possible.

Glossary

Activation: A state where the nervous system prepares the body for action. The heart rate increases, muscles tighten and attention focuses on potential problems or threats.

Aligned Beliefs: Beliefs that support the person you are becoming. These beliefs help you make choices that feel authentic, confident and consistent with your values.

Chronic Stress: A state where the body remains activated for long periods of time. Instead of returning to calm after a challenge, the nervous system stays on high alert.

Confirmation Bias: The brain's tendency to notice information that supports existing beliefs while ignoring information that challenges them.

Coregulation: The process by which one nervous system helps calm another. Humans naturally regulate through safe relationships, supportive conversations and emotional connection.

Hebbian Learning: Often summarized as *cells that fire together wire together.* When certain thoughts, emotions, or reactions repeat, the brain strengthens those pathways, making the pattern easier to repeat in the future.

Human Operating System (HOS): The internal system that shapes how a person thinks, feels and behaves. It includes the nervous system, emotional responses, beliefs and learned patterns that guide reactions to life.

Limbic Hijack: A moment when the emotional part of the brain reacts quickly and strongly before the thinking part of the brain can respond. This can lead to impulsive reactions or emotional overwhelm.

Neuroception: The nervous system's automatic process of scanning the environment for signals of safety or danger, often outside of conscious awareness.

Neuroscience: The scientific study of the brain, nervous system, and how they influence thoughts, emotions and behavior.

Nervous System: The network of nerves and brain structures that control how the body senses, responds and regulates itself.

Pattern Recognition: The brain's ability to detect familiar situations based on past experiences and quickly predict what might happen next.

Regulation: The process of helping the nervous system return to balance after stress or activation.

Regulation Strategies: Practices that help the body settle and return to balance. Examples include breathing, movement, body awareness and supportive connection.

Self-Sabotaging Behavior: Actions that unintentionally interfere with personal goals or well-being, often driven by old survival patterns or beliefs.

State-Dependent Behavior: The idea that a person's behavior changes depending on their nervous system state. When the body feels safe, choices tend to be thoughtful; when the body feels threatened, reactions become more automatic.

Survival Beliefs: Beliefs formed during emotionally intense experiences that helped a person cope or stay safe. These beliefs may continue guiding behavior long after the original situation has passed.

Survival Mind: The part of the mind focused on protection, threat detection and staying safe. It reacts quickly and prioritizes survival over curiosity or creativity.

Sympathetic Branch of the Nervous System: The part of the nervous system responsible for mobilizing the body for action. It increases alertness, energy and readiness during challenges.

Vagus Nerve: A major nerve that connects the brain to many organs in the body. It plays an important role in calming the nervous system and supporting regulation.

Wiser Mind: The part of the mind that becomes accessible when the nervous system is calm. It allows reflection, perspective, thoughtful decision-making and aligned choices.

www.ingramcontent.com/pod-product-compliance
Lightning Source LLC
LaVergne TN
LVHW010654110826
845149LV00014B/3082